The Wild Boy

Then suddenly, without warning, a blaze of light, a beacon, shone on one small corner of the wood just across the little meadow. The intensity of the light made my eyes sting. It was all I could do to keep from turning away, as if I beheld brightest day after the dark of total eclipse.

And just then, as the light of a new day began its first, faint glow, a strange form burst from the woods. It was as raw and pink as a newborn pig, but much larger, and it scudded across the meadow on all fours, a beast at once frightened and frightening in its wildness and the unexpectedness of its arrival.

**Other Point paperbacks
you will want to read:**

The Catalogue of the Universe
by Margaret Mahy

Double Trouble
by Barthe DeClements and Christopher Greimes

Nell's Quilt
by Susan Terris

A Band of Angels
by Julian Thompson

The Changeover: A Supernatural Romance
Margaret Mahy

point

BORN INTO LIGHT

Paul Samuel Jacobs

SCHOLASTIC INC.
New York Toronto London Auckland Sydney

ISBN 0-590-44765-3

12 11 10 9 8 7 6 5 4 3 2 1   0 1 2 3 4 5/9

To Marlie, Nora, and Jordan,
who have always liked to be
told stories.

BORN INTO LIGHT

1

By Morning's First Light

Children scorn me and that gives me pain, but I cannot blame them. Old age has transformed me, given me a monstrous visage. Deep crevices and bulging pockets of skin have made my face as weathered as a worn-out shoe. My eyelids droop like half-drawn window shades. My hair grows in irregular tufts, as stiff and wild as beach grass. My bones have become gnarled and twisted like the limbs of an ancient tree.

If that were all, I might not complain. But the lenses of my old, old eyes have clouded, so that the world seems to swim before me as if I were a diver in a milky sea. Yet my failing sight cannot shut out the view of my mind's eye. There, what I knew and saw when I was very young remains clear and sharp in memory's vision.

And that is fortunate, because, old as I am, I have a story to tell that requires an unclouded view of events that are more than 70 years away. There, in the distance of a lifetime, I can still see a perfect spring morning, when I was a boy of only 10, a very thorough boy, full of mischief and energy. I was not then the famous Roger Westwood, aged scientist and dignified winner of prizes, an ugly old man you might have seen receiving a medal from the President in the Rose Garden.

I was little Roger Westwood, small even for my age. My face was smooth, my hair dark, my body straight as a new nail. More than most boys of my years in that time and place I was closely watched and only recently allowed to roam free in whatever direction I might choose. Sometimes my wanderings would take me through the small New England town where we lived, with its train station and leaky water tower that filled the great steam engines before their great puff over the mountains. At other times, I would turn instead toward the forest that edged up against the grassy meadow behind our house. To me, the town, the hills, the countryside and forest seemed as boundless and infinitely enticing as the whole of the universe might look to an astronaut.

We were a little family for those days, just the three of us: Mother, my sister Charlotte, who was 14, and I. Before I knew him, my father had died in a horrible accident, one of those tragedies that were much more frequent then than now, in which large numbers perish like so many insects under the foot of an uncaring passerby. My father had been working for the railroad on a line that would shorten the westward route by boring straight through the mountains. But a tunnel collapse had buried him and 43 others.

Eventually the line, or part of it, was finished, built on tombstones, my mother often said. Our town and the railroad prospered. And our little family scraped by, living on the shavings. We had more than most, but still very little. Fortunately the house was Mother's, free of mortgage, a gift from her family. There was also a small sum every month from an inheritance, and a pittance more from the railroad.

If we suffered, I did not know it. Mother had what she called her economies. We had no horse. We chopped our own wood. If the roof leaked, Mother climbed up herself to patch it.

Our house was small, well made, but with too many rooms for its size, so that it was like a beehive. We all had our own little chambers to squeeze into. The only exception was the kitchen, a vast expanse of room where we spent much of our time together, sitting on cushioned chairs around a great round oaken table that could accommodate a dozen diners.

We kept a garden, less for the necessities of life than for a few of its luxuries. Every summer we would harvest a crop of sweet corn, french beans, grapes and berries, and tomatoes so large and swollen that they burst warm through their skins when you bit into them.

We built a tall fence around the garden to keep the deer out. But we did not treat those soft, spotted creatures as our enemies. Mother took pity upon them and often fed them from her own hand. Whatever the season, they would come out of the woods at the earliest hour of a new day to search through a pile of cooking debris my mother had left for them just outside the kitchen door. I would race out to greet them. Tame as they were, when faced with my boisterous affection, the startled deer would plunge back into the forest. I would follow in such frenzy that it was a wonder they bothered to come back again. Yet they did return, regularly, stags and does and fawns alike. And every morning, I began my day by looking for them from the window by my bed, from which I could look out at the forest.

On this particular late spring morning, the sun seemed to me particularly slow in rising. Perhaps a granite cloud had stood in its path and blocked its progress across the sky. Already I could hear the sounds of our household's rising, the bustling of my mother and sister as they began preparations for a new day. But I was under instructions to stay abed until first light. I lay in my bed restless for dawn to show itself. I kept reaching over and pulling back the curtains, but dawn did not come. Even the birds were silent, showing that they had a good deal more patience than I.

Then suddenly, without warning, a blaze of light, a beacon, shone on one small corner of the wood just across the little meadow. The intensity of the light made my eyes sting. It was all I could do to keep from turning away, as if I beheld brightest day after the dark of total eclipse. It seemed a miracle that I did not scald my eyes. The beacon dimmed, giving off a cloud of white smoke, like a candle that had blown out.

And just then, as the light of a new day began its first, faint glow, a strange form burst from the woods. It was as raw and pink as a newborn pig, but much larger, and it scudded across the meadow on all fours, a beast at once frightened and frightening in its wildness and the unexpectedness of its arrival. At that moment, I heard the slap of the screen door and saw my sister, Charlotte, race into the clearing to meet the onrushing creature, which braked and then rose up on its back legs.

Taking the scene in from my window, I was startled and terrified at what seemed a threat to my sister. But my initial surprise was nothing to what I felt when I suddenly realized that the wild thing that had burst from the forest was not an animal at all, but a fully formed human being — a boy of about my size. He stood there for one brief second in our usually quiet meadow, without a stitch of clothing, until my sister caught him and wrapped him in a great rag of an old blanket. She picked him up as easily as she would a favored lamb, and carried him into the house, where Mother and I were waiting.

2

Taming of the Beast

He was as much animal as boy, thrashing violently in a vain effort to break loose of the blanket that my sister had swaddled him in. From his mouth came a mixture of whimpers and cries, but nothing that resembled speech. When I approached to take a closer look, he bared his teeth and snapped at me and growled from deep within his throat with all the menace of a guard dog.

"Don't let him bite you!" Mother cried out. "He might be hydrophobic."

How Charlotte managed to hold him and avoid a bite, I do not know. But hold him she did, with her long, wiry arms surrounding him and pinning him to her.

"I have him firm," Charlotte said calmly.

"Throw him in the shed!" Mother said. "We'll have to lock him up there for the time being. He seems more dog than boy." But when she approached to help Charlotte, the creature renewed his struggle, kicking and snapping so that my sister seemed on the verge of losing him. I rushed to Mother's side and pulled her back. As she retreated, the boy seemed to quiet down again.

"Get him some food, Mama," Charlotte commanded, and Mother, so strong and wise and formidable in most situations, became strangely dutiful. She poured a small amount of milk into a bowl and, holding it out at arm's length, offered it to the boy.

I wondered how the boy could accept this offering, shackled as he was in my sister's arms. But Mother put the bowl on the floor and stood back in the corner of the kitchen next to the great woodstove where I cowered, terror-struck, but too filled with curiosity and concern to exit the room.

Released by Charlotte, the boy knelt over the bowl and lapped up the milk. He scarcely looked up when I let out a laugh at the sight of a full-grown boy drinking from a bowl like some puppy or kitten. When the milk was gone, he retreated back again to Charlotte's arms, where he seemed calmed by the food and the warm comfort of our house. Wrapped up again in the blanket, he yelped a bit, licked his lips, and dozed off.

My sister lifted him easily, as if he were not made of flesh at all but of some lighter, hollow substance. Without a hint of strain, she followed Mother into my room, where the two of them stretched this animal-boy across my bed.

Relaxed and softened by sleep, his face lost its beast-like appearance. He had dark, dark hair that covered his ears and spilled over the collar of blanket that still surrounded him. I sucked in a deep breath when I saw how much he looked like me. At that precise moment, as if reading my own thoughts, Mother said, "Why, he might be Roger's very twin." It must have been an illusion, but the more I stared, the more the resemblance grew, as if little by little, he was being transformed into an exact replica of me.

"Roger," Mother said softly, her fears vanished with the milk in the bowl, "run and fetch Dr. Jensen. Quickly, now!"

A path along the edge of the meadow led to the doctor's house, perhaps a half mile from our own. It was the largest house in the village and served as both home and office. I sprinted the whole distance, arriving breathlessly at his door, next to which hung his shingle, a brightly polished brass plate that proclaimed, "Charles M. Jensen, M.D." I pulled on the bell cord again and again until he came to the door. He was a tall man, who seemed shrunken in his clothes. His lean, sharp features might have been frightening to a child, except he blunted their effect with a gentle smile and soft voice.

"What seems to be the matter?" he asked.

"We found a wild boy!" I blurted out. "Mother says to come quick!"

He moved back into the house long enough to grab a dark satchel. After running all the way back, Dr. Jensen stood in our kitchen, warily watching the boy. Dressed in some discarded clothing of mine, the boy hunkered down next to Charlotte's chair. As we talked, his eyes moved from one of us to the other, as if he could follow our conversation.

"I'd swear he was one of your own, Elizabeth," Dr.

Jensen said. "He looks remarkably healthy. What's puzzling is that I cannot see a cut or scratch on him. His skin is like a baby's. I've read accounts of wild children, raised in the woods by animals or managing to survive on their own. Feral children, we call them. But how might he have escaped such an existence without even a scratch, free of vermin, so clean and uncalloused?"

The boy grunted as if he were trying to imitate our speech. When I, for the second time now, laughed aloud at him, he growled and moved toward me only to be tugged back by my sister, as if he were a vicious dog, restrained by his master.

"What's to be done with him?" Charlotte asked. "Can we keep him here with us?"

"I would not advise it, even if you had the means," said the doctor. "You might tame a feral child, but he'd never be more than an ape with clothes, forever mute, incapable of intelligent thought or expression. More than an animal, he would be, but less than a moron. I can imagine no creature in all of nature more pathetic than such an animalized human being as this one you have found."

The boy growled deep in his throat and I sensed that he had become dangerous again, as if a spring trap deep within him had been stretched and set. In that instant, he seemed capable of terrible destruction.

Charlotte sensed the danger, too, and she reached over and petted the boy's dark mane, a gesture that soothed and quieted him.

"If he doesn't stay with us, at least until his kin can be found, what will happen to him?" Mother asked.

"There is a home for the deranged not far from here," Dr. Jensen said in a muffled voice, as if he hoped that the boy would not hear. "I have had occasion to visit there of late."

Charlotte burst into tears. "Such a place of despair," she cried.

"Then you know the home," the doctor nodded glumly.

And indeed we did know it. One of my earliest memories was following a large, bearded man through the dark, fetid rooms of the county home, where the insane and defective, unwanted children and adults, were kept out of view of the rest of society.

Each year at Thanksgiving we would go there, with meats and pies, fruits and loaves of bread still steaming. A small number of children waited for us, seated about a table in a shuttered room. There was a clamor of clattering plates and spoons. Those children who did eat would do so with their hands or devour the food directly from the plates. But others, eyes sunken and foreheads marred by scars and scabs, would shrink away, only to have the matrons thrust heaping spoons into their unwilling mouths. What was not spit back or dribbled over a chin was more choked down than swallowed.

I asked myself what evil deeds had these children done to be imprisoned in such a place.

I looked at our wild boy and wondered if we would have to visit him there in the county home.

"It is a backward, terribly backward institution," Dr. Jensen said. "But perhaps we could interest a medical school in Boston in the boy's case, and then the county home would be only a way station. A true wild child is a rare specimen. He would be most prized."

"I won't have it," Mother said, raising her voice as

if to rebuke the doctor. "As long as I have a scrap of food to provide, he may share in it."

As with many of Mother's decisions, this one was made in an instant and blurted out without a thought for the possible consequences. Once said, she was determined to do whatever was required. Dr. Jensen smiled and took one of her hands in the two of his, as if to congratulate her for her decision.

"Will he be my brother?" I asked.

"Yes," Mother said. "Unless someone comes to claim him as their own kin, he will be one of ours."

I was bewildered and yet pleased at the same time. In one stroke, I had gained a brother and an odd sort of pet, a wild primate that would need to be tamed and even housebroken.

My friends would be impressed. They were sure to be terrified of him, as I was. I hoped that their awe might rub off and be transferred to me. If only I could be certain that he would not attack me, then my pleasure would be complete.

3

The Creature in the Pond

Through most of that first day, the boy slept. And I wasted no time getting off to the grove where I had seen the blaze of light that morning. The woods there had been transformed. A circle of trees lay broken, radiating from a brown circle some twenty feet across that was burned into the ground. The trees were arranged like the spokes of a wheel — the burned spot its hub. The place had a strange odor, like that of wooden matches in the first second of flash into flame.

In and around the burnt-brown circle, I found pieces of a strange material, a shiny gray substance that seemed metallic but disintegrated into a fine powder in my hands. Without touching it, I looked at one of the largest pieces, which was about the size of my hand. The fragment was curved gently and grooved, as if it had been made up of pieces of rope as thick as a finger.

I realized at once that the metal that turned to powder with a touch might be connected to the arrival of the wild boy, and I was so excited by my discovery that I tried to pick up the largest piece, only to feel it turn to dust in my hand. I began to look around for more evidence when I saw a flash of light above the trees in the distance, like a meteor across the sky. This was followed seconds later by a noise that sounded like hot iron plunged into water. I had heard a similar hiss of scorching heat at the metal shop in the railroad yard, where the burly smith repaired the iron parts needed to keep the stock rolling along its way.

Following the trail of light, I ran along a deer path that took me up to the pond, no less than a mile from where I had been standing. When I arrived at the near shore, all was still except for my gasping for breath. It was unusually quiet, as if all the birds and small animals had been frightened away. I had raced the whole distance, and it took me several minutes before I could breathe easily again. I stood at a sandy beach where my sister and I came to wade and swim in the summer, when the pond at last grew warm. The two of us would sometimes hike here in other seasons as well, but Mother warned us that if we went in the pond before it was time, we would certainly die of the cold. Ignoring her, we sometimes would walk out into the water when it was still so chilled that it would make my ankles ache. That was the extent of our defiance of our mother's orders, however.

She worried that we might drown, a fear that would have grown if she knew of the time that Charlotte had rescued me when I walked out too far and sank like a stone beneath the surface. My sister had pumped the water out of me until, after a spasm of coughing, I managed to tell her that I could breathe very well on my own.

Most of the shore was swampy and lined with clusters of cattails that grew along the pond's mucky edges. I began to walk around, feeling the muddy path suck at my feet. The growth along the shoreline blocked my view of the water, so now and then I stepped out into the pond beyond the brush and cattails, ignoring the water and mud that engulfed my shoes.

The search was haphazard. I did not know what I was looking for or where I might find whatever it was. Less than halfway around the pond, I noticed an object floating among a scattering of lily pads. To reach it I would have to wade out into the water, in violation of my mother's strictest orders. I was still too fearful of drowning to try to swim out by myself. But with a long branch in my hand, I waded out as far as I dared and began to poke at the thing. I hoped that with my stick I could maneuver the object back to the shore for a closer look. As I poked at it, however, it only floated further away.

Yet I was close enough to see the object, fleshy pink where it was not covered by a crust of metallic gray. It was like a great, bloated salamander, with curled limbs, but without a tail. Its rounded head was dominated by large blue, almost black, eyes, and a flattened piglike nose.

I wanted desperately for Dr. Jensen to see this thing, because I was certain that only he could properly explain it. So I plunged for it among the water lilies, only to find myself in water over my head. As I thrashed about trying to regain my footing and the shore, the creature bobbed away. It seemed to sink beneath the glimmering surface of the pond.

Shivering — my teeth chattering — as cold as a melting icicle, I somehow made it to the path and began to run for home. I must have burst out of the woods in the same way the wild boy had done earlier that day, but no one raced out to meet me. I ran through the house wildly looking for Mother. She and Charlotte were in my room. The boy lay in my bed, my mother's hand on his forehead.

"What happened?" Mother asked. Her voice was calm, but from her face, I could tell that I must have been a frightening sight, wet and spattered with mud.

"I fell in the pond," I said, my jaws chattering so that it was all I could do to say even that much.

"Help me get this boy to bed," Mother said to Charlotte. I was surprised she said no more than that. I had broken several of Mother's rules. I had ventured to the pond on my own; I had entered the water in a season when it was dangerously cold; I had tumbled in over my head and thereby narrowly escaped drowning. Only the strange pink creature, floating lifelessly in the water, could justify all I had done in defiance of my mother's code of conduct. I would need to explain everything quickly to avoid certain punishment, I thought.

"I saw something terrible," I managed to say. In a whisper, I added, "A monster."

"Hush, now, Roger boy, hush," Mother said. "There will be time to talk later." What a pitiable sight I must have been to escape even a hint of wrath after breaking Mother's rules. Silently, with Charlotte's help, Mother dressed me in warm clothes and put me, still shivering, into my bed, next to my warm-bodied twin. I cannot remember falling asleep. Surely my dreams included visions of that pink amphibian, bobbing in the water and turning toward me with that dark and sulfurous eye.

4

The Light of the Second Day

I woke up to the dawn of another day when the wild boy began pinching my nose.

"Stop that!" I squealed as loudly as I could. The boy retracted his hand. For the first time, it was I who had frightened him.

"What's the matter?" yelled my mother as she raced into the room.

"He grabbed my nose and I couldn't breathe," I said, with only a little exaggeration.

"Nose," the wild boy said distinctly. "Nose."

For the briefest second, Mother and I were frozen by the word, as if one of the neighbors' pigs had suddenly begun to speak to us.

"Then he can talk," Mother said as she pulled me to her and hugged me affectionately, as if I were somehow responsible for this miracle of speech.

"But he doesn't know what it means," I said.

At that moment the boy began to finger his own nose, repeating almost endlessly his first and only word. "Nose. Nose. Nose."

Whether that was the true beginning of his speech or whether he was simply recalling what he had once tucked away in a deep pocket of his brain, out of the way but not forgotten, I do not know for certain, even now. But before that second day had scarcely begun, he had risen out of infancy or imbecility with a single word.

No greater transformation, no larger miracle of life can be imagined. It was only much later in life that I realized that every child, except for the most sadly defective, undergoes the same transformation in the first few years of life, from mute animal to speaking human. It is, after all, speech that sets our species apart, makes us intelligent beings, and defines our humanity.

And with the birth of speech, the wild boy, my new brother, entered the race of men.

I leaped out of bed and began to dress myself, full of hope that this second day of the wild boy's life with us would be as adventurous as the first. I was dressed and at the breakfast table even before Charlotte guided the boy to a chair and tried to convince him to sit in it, rather than knock it over and stomp upon it, as if it were an enemy to be vanquished.

"No, no," she said. "Like this." And she demonstrated with an unusual amount of ladylike gentility just how civilized creatures arranged their bodies before partaking of a meal.

"Show him, Roger," she pleaded.

I hunkered down near Charlotte, close enough for the boy to see me, but too far for him to launch another attack upon my nose. I raised up in imitation of a bear rearing up on its hind legs, and then I sidled over to my own chair and plopped down.

"Oh, won't you do it naturally?" Charlotte implored me. So once again, I dropped down, rose to my feet, and then, shouting "Sit!" plummeted to my chair.

To our astonishment and delight, the boy followed my example. Charlotte and I laughed and applauded. To that, the boy also began laughing and applauding, so uproariously that he tipped his chair backward and fell to the ground.

I laughed all the harder, but Charlotte gathered him in her arms. He was whimpering with great tears leaking down from his eyes, more baby than wild beast.

Seated again, he picked up the bowl before him and turned it up over his head, as if wondering why there was no milk in it, as there had been the day before.

Mother brought a cauldron of porridge to the table and a pitcher of cream. When she tried to take the bowl from the wild boy's hand, he would not let it go. Suddenly, he released it and grabbed instead for the pitcher, spilling the cream all over the table and then jumping up in his chair so that he could lap it up.

"No!" Mother shouted. And then, with more patience than she would have shown me had I been the one licking cream off the table, she added, "That is not the way we drink milk in this house."

She grabbed him up in her strong arms and began to carry him away from the table, when suddenly he blurted out, "Milk!" almost as if it were a question. Mother was so startled that she let him go. He charged to the table, putting his face at the point where a dribble of the white fluid was spilling over the edge to the floor. "Milk," he said.

By the end of breakfast, Mother and Charlotte had convinced the boy to lap his milk up from his bowl rather than first pouring it from the container and about the room. And he had added half a dozen words, including "Mama" and "Shara" for Charlotte to his growing vocabulary. Me, he called, "Boy," a word he also used to describe himself.

After breakfast, he squatted down in the corner of the kitchen nearest the stove, and in that no doubt uncomfortable position, managed to fall asleep.

I told Mother in detail about my previous day's experience, about the burnt circle and the shooting star that led me to the salamanderlike creature I found in the pond.

"Show me," Mother said.

I retraced my steps, showing her first the burnt ground and then leading her up to the pond along the same deer path I had taken the day before.

"This is where I found the thing," I said. "The monster. There." I pointed toward the lily pads.

"You stay right here, Roger," she said. Taking me by surprise, she carefully took off her shoes and placed them near me, on the high ground above the pond. She then walked down to the muddy edge. She waded out into the water, bending low and using her dress to scoop through the plants, as if she were a fisherman trying to net a large fish.

She must have been very cold by the time she came out, several minutes later. The light wind set her shivering.

"You do believe me, Mama," I said.

"Yes," she answered. "I know you did not make that up." I clung to her wet, muddy dress as we walked down together.

In the burnt circle, Charlotte and the boy were waiting for us. I showed them all how the metallic pieces crumbled to the touch. After watching with interest, Mother seemed cold and weary.

"Let's go home, now, children," she said.

"Where is your home?" I asked the boy.

"Home," he said as plainly as I. "Home." But as he said it he was looking down at the fragmented pieces that lay on the ground. And I found myself laughing again at this fool of a creature, this orphan delivered of the woods and born into light.

At dinner, we sat again around the table, more or less patiently waiting for Mother to bring the kettles of food from the iron stove that stood against the far wall of the kitchen. The boy had taken his seat without prompting, and Charlotte was giving him his first lesson in the use of normal kitchen utensils. The lesson did not go well. He seemed to prefer clinking his knife and fork together rather than putting them to their intended purpose. When Mother was finally seated, we handed our plates to her to be filled with the plain but abundant meal.

Without any urging, the boy imitated us and soon had a plate of potatoes before him, still steaming hot from the stove. I began to attack mine with my knife and fork, but he, forsaking the tableware, began assaulting his dinner with his hands. He let out a howl as terrifying as that of a wolf.

"The poor boy has burned his mouth," Mother said as if to translate his animal sound into English. She rose from her chair but failed to reach the boy before Charlotte was at his side, coaxing him to eat in small bites.

"Hot," Charlotte said, as she might have spoken to an infant or a kitten. "Hot."

"Hot," he bleated.

"Potato," she explained. "Potato hot." She broke his food into smaller pieces and then stuck one with a fork and held it up to blow on. He soon got the idea, but continued to think that every piece needed blowing on, even after everything had cooled. The boy ate with a ferocious appetite, as I did.

"I want more potatoes," I said unceremoniously.

"You mean, 'Please pass the potatoes,' " Charlotte said, tossing me a spiteful glance.

"Keep your nose out of other people's business," I said.

"Nose!" piped up the boy.

"You keep out of it, too!" I barked. "You don't even know what we're talking about!"

"Shara nose," he said, fondly, pointing to my sister's face, which already carried the long straight nose characteristic of Mother and her offspring.

Charlotte blushed.

"Boy milk," he now said with special urgency.

"Roger milk," I demanded, taking pains to imitate his exact manner of speech and then laughing.

"That's enough out of you, young man," Mother said. She grabbed my arm and pulled me from the table. She left me to sit by myself in a corner of the room by the stove.

I knew at once that my mother was right to be angry. I was mocking the wild boy and taking unmistakable pleasure in it. Sitting by the stove, the room felt un-

24

usually warm to me. I was flushed and humiliated, but at the same time angry at this intruder who sat comfortably at my table with my family, all of them acting as if I did not exist at all.

I saw him again as an alien being, and I found myself feeling about him what a dog must feel instinctively about a cat; or what a cat feels about a bird. He was a rival, a member of another species. I wanted to sneak up on him and pounce on him.

In the middle of these spiteful and malicious thoughts, I looked over to see the boy spear a potato from his plate with his fork. He held the fork upright before him, admiring the vegetable as much as he might a gold nugget or a jewel. Then he moved his mouth to the fork and began to gnaw at the potato. He paused after each bite to enjoy the new shape he had left behind. I longed to eat a potato in just that way. No potato ever seemed as delicious.

I found myself looking forward to the days ahead of us, to showing him off to my friends and to teaching him all the proper ways of civilization. And maybe, I thought, he would have some tricks to teach me, too.

Charlotte did not admire the way the boy had eaten his potato and did her best to show him how it ought to be done with a knife and fork. He did not take to this quickly, but she repeated her demonstration over and over until finally Mother said, "I think the boy has learned enough for one night."

"Shara," said the boy, as if to reassure my sister that he had not run out of patience even if our mother had.

In the days that followed, it was Charlotte who spent the most time with the boy, correcting his childish speech and improving his manners.

When I could, on the other hand, I tried to run off with him. I liked nothing better than to tackle him from behind, to race and wrestle and roughhouse with him. So hardfought was our play that it was a wonder that neither of us was hurt. To my infinite pleasure, the boy tried to imitate me. I ran across the meadow; he followed. I vaulted a low wooden fence and so did he, as faultlessly as I, although he had never practiced. He followed me up trees so high that I was not sure either of us would be able to climb back down again.

We scrambled through crawl spaces under houses, up and over boxcars at the train siding, through great brambles, and over rounded hilltops. We tumbled, rolled, reeled, and careened through the world I already knew, and that quickly became his world, too.

He was becoming more human every day.

5

Christened and Tested

The wild boy's speech continued to grow with remarkable speed. And the day came, very quickly, when it was hard to remember that he was once unable to speak like one of us. For a long time, however, he pronounced words in a strange way, as if he had come from another country where English was not spoken at all. He had, Dr. Jensen declared, a European accent.

The doctor had become a frequent visitor to our house since the boy's first arrival. He was keeping a notebook, he told us, as a record of the boy's progress. It was the doctor's theory that the boy had been lost or abandoned. Perhaps he had fallen or been dropped from a passing train.

"There may have been others," he said, nodding toward Mother as if to remind her that the two of them had talked about this possibility before. It was late on a summer morning, the air already so warm and heavy that it was difficult to breathe. We sat in the kitchen and listened to Dr. Jensen — all of us except Charlotte, who seemed unaffected by the heat and was outside working in the garden. As the doctor spoke, the boy sat on the floor of the kitchen examining his bare feet and not following the conversation.

"I believe now that he was left here, and the terror of awaking, cold and alone in a strange wood, must have shocked his brain," the doctor said. "His mind was wiped as clean as a slate at the schoolhouse. But deep within his mind, he retained a dim memory of everything he had learned before. And that explains why within just a few weeks he can speak as well as any other child his age. I would guess that he is German-born but already skilled in English."

Suddenly the doctor turned to the boy as if he was about to pounce on him. *"Kannst du Deutsch sprechen?"* Dr. Jensen said. But the wild boy paid him no attention and continued to study the way the toes attach to the feet.

"Perhaps the German language will come back to him later," the doctor said. He turned to Mother and looked straight into her eyes, not shifting his gaze as he spoke. "Your kindness and patience have helped to transform him. You have thawed his mind with the warmth that you have provided him."

Mother blushed and pulled back a stray lock of her brown hair, a delicate gesture for a woman with rough, strong hands.

Tiring of their talk, but too hot to consider any energetic activity, I slipped off my shoes and began contemplating the miracle of my own feet.

"It's Charlotte and Roger who have taken hold of him," she said.

"You are much too modest, Elizabeth," the doctor said, reaching out both of his smooth, fine hands to her. "You have done so well with him. Are you sure you are prepared to attempt to care for another?"

Puzzled, I looked up at the two of them.

"Let me see the little girl first, and then we all will decide," Mother said.

Holding her hands in his, the doctor said, "Once you see her, you will find it very difficult not to take her away with you."

Mother returned the doctor's gaze in a way that I was unaccustomed to see my mother look at anyone. I thought of her as very old, although she was just a few years past 30. Now she was acting like a girl, young and in some ways foolish.

She turned in my direction. "Roger, why don't you take the boy out with you and play. It will be cooler in the woods than it is here in the house."

"Elizabeth, you must put a name on him. It has been more than a month now," Dr. Jensen said. "You can't continue to call him 'boy.' "

"I've always supposed that someone would come to claim him from us," Mother said. "It seemed wrong to give him a name not really his own."

"Let's call him 'Benjamin,' " I said, inspired by a book of sayings that the doctor had lately given us. " 'Benjamin Westwood' is a very good name."

"A fine choice," the doctor said. "The name is from the Hebrew. 'Child of the right hand,' it means. To be right-handed was thought to be fortunate. A fine name for any creature rescued by this loving family."

Mother agreed. Properly christened at last, Benjamin, my brother Ben, and I ran out toward the woods.

In the clearing still imprinted with the burnt circle, several of my playmates stood at strict attention while Jackson Stone, the village bully, paraded in front of them. When Jackson spotted the two of us, he said sharply, "You two can join the rest of them." He pointed to a line he had drawn with a stick across the dusty ground. "Snap to it," he said. "And stand at attention."

Ben hurried into place alongside the others. He appeared grateful to be included in the game. But I moved reluctantly, kicking billows of dust up from the dry earth. Jackson, who stood a full head taller than any of us, threatened me with his large fists. "Move, private," he said. "Or I'll bloody your nose for you."

I might have made a run for it, back to the house and into the protection of my mother's arms. But then Jackson would only have taunted me with that later, as I had seen him do to other boys of my age. And I could not abandon Ben to Jackson's wretched little private army. So I took my place on the line and waited as the bully paraded up and down, occasionally punching one of us hard in the kidneys from behind if we did not maintain a correct military posture. As we stood there, the air seemed to weigh down upon my shoulders. I longed to shift my weight or to change positions entirely, but Jackson would not allow that.

I was soon drenched in my own sweat, but did not dare to wipe away the rivulet that streamed down my forehead. I thought that Jackson would soon tire of his boring game, but when I tried to suggest a more active game, I was thanked with a solid punch to the kidney.

"Stand tall," he commanded. "Eyes front. No swaying there. Straight and steady or you'll pay for it."

Just as I thought I could put up with the game no longer and that I would rather risk walking away than stand still another minute, I heard the dreadful sound of a body hitting the ground heavily beside me. It was Ben, who had fainted dead away.

"See what you've done!" I screamed at Jackson. He and the others seemed as surprised by my outburst as they were by the sight of Ben sprawled on the ground. Ben quickly showed signs of consciousness, then bolted upright with a confused expression on his face. "I fell asleep," he said, as if to explain what had happened and apologize for it.

But my fury was so great that I scarcely cared that Ben showed every sign of recovery. I hurled myself at Jackson, my arms flailing against him, and actually succeeded in knocking him to the ground, to our mutual surprise. I kept up the attack as he lay there on his back, until he was able to push me away. Getting to his feet, he smiled, a great grin full of crooked, yellow teeth. His eyes grew small and he spat into the dust.

"I'll show you," he said. "Pipsqueak." And with that he punched me squarely in the nose, and he would have struck me again, except that blood spurted from my nostrils.

Behind me, Ben had risen to his feet, and in imitation of Jackson, he held up his fists, striking a prizefighter's pose. The two boys plunged at one another, little Ben against the older giant. The bully delivered two quick jabs to Ben's face, but the blows did not stop Ben from moving even closer to Jackson and grabbing the larger boy about the waist.

I am not sure how Ben was able to do it, but he

lifted Jackson over his head and threw him ten feet, as if it were no more trouble than tossing a piece of firewood.

Jackson scrambled to his feet and ran off into the woods, the sounds of our laughter pursuing him and doing more injury than his fall.

"I'll get you!" we heard him call out, not very convincingly. "I'll get you little pipsqueaks!"

When Ben and I reached home, Mother was alone in the kitchen, already at work on our evening meal. She was stripping husks from corn harvested from our own garden.

"What happened to the two of you?" she asked. We were covered with a grime of dust and sweat, and my nose was caked with blood.

"Nothing," I replied as nonchalantly as I could.

"Nothing?" she said. "What about that nose? I hope you haven't broken it. Roger Westwood, tell me what has happened!"

"I walked into a tree," I said.

Ben looked sincerely puzzled. "I did not see you walk into a tree," he said.

"You must have been looking the other way when I did," I said.

"Oh," he said. "I am surprised I did not see that." But he had to know I was not telling the truth.

Mother let the subject drop. If she had insisted, I would have told her what had happened. But the code of my boyhood did not permit the telling of tales. Mother understood that, but Ben could not. He knew no code of conduct other than truthfulness. His knowing that I had lied to Mother only added to the torment of the morning.

6

A Creature Rescued

After cleaning up, we gathered for our midday meal. Mother seemed distracted and grew impatient with Benjamin.

"Sit up, Ben," Mother commanded him. It was still his habit to put his face as close to plate or bowl as possible to avoid dropping morsels of food over the edge of the table and to the floor, where he was forbidden to recover them.

"Sit up?" Ben asked. "I can stand up. I can sit down. But what does it mean to sit up?"

"It means to sit straight," said Charlotte, trying to be helpful.

"But when I sit, my body is folded in two places. If I unfold it, I am no longer sitting, but standing. How can I sit and be straight?"

"With your back straight," Charlotte explained again.

"My back is straight," Ben said. "It cannot fold. It is always straight."

"It means to sit the way Roger is sitting," Mother said in an effort to end the discussion. I beamed my superiority in the same way that a native takes pleasure in thinking himself better than foreigners with scant knowledge of local custom.

Although Ben had more or less learned the use of knives, forks, and spoons, he could not understand their necessity. Now that he was sitting straight in his chair, they seemed especially clumsy and unnecessary.

"Why do we use these tools to eat?" Ben asked Mother.

"For cleanliness," Mother explained.

"But we must wash our hands before we eat."

"If you used your hands, *they* would be dirty," Mother said.

"Then I could wash my hands again after I eat," Ben said.

"All that washing of hands, if you don't use knives and forks," Mother said.

"All that washing of knives and forks," replied Ben.

Mother for once seemed exasperated with Ben. "It is just the way we do things," she said.

"Then I will do so, too," he said, sitting as straight as a folded body would permit and gripping his knife and fork so tightly that it would have been a struggle to pry them from him.

Mother laughed, and when Dr. Jensen returned to our house in the late afternoon, she recounted the entire conversation, much to the doctor's amusement.

"He has a point, you know," the doctor said. "Few people on earth bother with such implements. Many of those who do, use sticks to handle food and not metal instruments. And yet a man or woman in our society who cannot deftly handle knife and fork is considered a base being, an animal. The whole matter has nothing to do with what truly distinguishes us from our crude cousins, the apes."

Whenever Dr. Jensen came by, Mother dropped her work to sit and talk with him, often in the kitchen and sometimes in the little parlor we used only for special occasions, at Christmastime or Easter or when the schoolteacher, Mrs. Winfield, came to call. My mother was honored by the physician's attention to Ben and our family.

On this occasion, however, there was no time for talk. Pulling a large gold watch from a vest pocket, the doctor impatiently declared, "It is time that we go. We are expected."

"Go where?" I asked, only to be ignored in the bustle of movement toward the doctor's horse and carriage, which waited for us outside. But we had not traveled far when we turned off on a familiar rutted road that I knew ended at the county home — the place that Dr. Jensen spoke of as the "home for the deranged," but that the children of our town, in whispering tones, called "the madhouse."

It was a two-story brick building with few adornments. What paint there was, on shutters and the big front door, was peeling. Despite the heat, the shutters were closed, and had there been a breeze it would have been locked out as an intruder.

Dr. Jensen rapped the heavy brass knocker of the worn wooden door.

As the door swung open, the house gasped out a faintly fetid breath. I recognized the man who greeted us, a large, bearded fellow dressed in shirtsleeves. "So good of all of you to come," he said, smiling at the adults but sending sneers in the direction of the children.

We followed him into a dank hallway and through a second door that opened into a shabby sitting room, where a woman wearing a large bonnet waited for us. "This is the one who found *her*," the bearded man said.

"I'm Mrs. Dublin," the woman explained as she removed her bonnet, allowing us to see that she was a very old woman indeed. "I found her, or I should say more properly that it was the girl who found me. It was already dark and I was just sitting down to supper when I saw a face at the window. And, of course, I let her in. Who would not have let her in, please tell me."

Mrs. Dublin's voice quavered, her head, her hands, her whole body trembled as she spoke. "I did the best I could for her, but she would not let me touch her. She even tried to bite me, you see. The poor creature. There was not much I could do, not at my age, living alone as I do. The next day, when my housekeeper came, I sent her to fetch Dr. Jensen, and we brought the girl here." Mrs. Dublin was sobbing into a lace handkerchief, which filled the air with a sweet perfume. Mother and Dr. Jensen tried to comfort her, as if she were an injured child who needed soothing and quieting.

The doctor turned to the bearded man, whose face was frozen into a toothful grin. He looked like a child who had been caught at some act of mischief and was betrayed by a smile. "Take us to her at once!"

"Just as you please," the man said. We trailed after

him through the narrow maze of corridors and up a cramped staircase to the floor above. In the darkest hallway, in the innermost part of the building, the little man fumbled with a set of keys and opened a door into a tiny chamber, far too small for us all to go in.

"It's a dungeon!" Charlotte cried.

"Dungeons are underground," I corrected her.

"A dungeon is a prison," Ben said. "Is this a prison?"

Our guide lit a candle and walked inside, followed by Dr. Jensen. From the doorway we could see a small child, huddled in a corner, wrapped in a blanket even on this hottest of days. Every bit of her was shrouded, except for her eyes, which were wide open and frightened. Mrs. Dublin, who stood behind me outside the room, began waving her perfumed handkerchief and sobbing. Mother rushed past us and into the chamber.

"We can't let her stay here, Charles," Mother blurted out.

"Then take her home with you," Dr. Jensen said softly. "I thought you would want to. I have made the necessary arrangements."

He lifted the child, still swaddled in her blanket, and carried her out of that miserable building and into the light of late afternoon. Outside, the blanket fallen away from her gaunt face, I could see that her hair was dull and matted. A faintly musty smell seemed to have followed after her. Through the whole time, she had not made a sound, not even a whimper.

Mother held the child in her arms as we crowded again into the carriage.

"You will have to pay for it, if you take it with you," the bearded man shouted after us.

"For the girl?" Dr. Jensen said in disbelief.

"No, no, not the girl. She belongs to Mrs. Dublin, who naturally enough wants no payment. For the blanket! They are costly to replace."

Gently, the doctor unwrapped the blanket from around the girl. It was a tattered, foul thing. Dr. Jensen rolled it into a ball and flung it at the bearded man, who stood quite still as if stunned by the blow.

The doctor clucked the horse forward.

"We forgot to ask Mrs. Dublin what we should call the child," Mother said.

"Her name is Nell," the doctor replied. "Nell Westwood, from this day forward, I think."

Despite the rocking and jolting of the carriage, little Nell dozed, and soon we were home.

7

The Gift of the Lamb

For several days, Nell scarcely moved from a cot that Mother put together on the floor of her room. Not only was she mute, but she did not seem to respond to us at all, as if a worm had bored its way into her brain and left her awake but senseless. The thin, sickly creature hardly had the strength to eat. Mother and Charlotte were forced to take turns feeding her with a spoon. We kept the windows and doors open wide through the heat of the day, and if a breeze came up, it would lift the curtains of the room and send them fluttering like flags in the moving air.

The kind treatment had its effect: a faint blush rose in her cheeks, her black hair shone from regular brushing. Now that she was with us, she was peaceful, and she always wore a faint smile that made me think of pictures I had seen of angels.

"I am afraid that Nell is a cretin," Dr. Jensen explained to us on the evening of her third day with our family. "One day we will understand this disease and perhaps be able to prevent its ill effects. Now we can only make her life as pleasant as possible, while we have her."

The next morning, the doctor surprised us by stopping by our house early in the morning, which was not his usual practice. Nell still slept, but the rest of us were stirring, and still in our nightclothes, Ben and Charlotte and I followed him outside, where we found a playful lamb. The doctor left us to pet the animal and emerged from the house a few minutes later with Nell in his arms. The lamb was cavorting like a kitten in the meadow behind the house as we chased after him. Dr. Jensen placed Nell on the ground, and we stopped to watch as she struggled to her feet and limped toward us. We held the lamb as still as we could until Nell could reach us and throw her arms around the neck of that pungent little animal.

"Better than the finest medicine," Dr. Jensen explained to Mother. And he was right. The lamb proved to be just the tonic that Nell needed. The fresh air, the exercise, and an improved appetite all served to strengthen the sickly girl. Soon she was able to chase after Ben and me in our ramblings in town and forest.

We kept the lamb in a pen we constructed next to the garden behind the house. It became a ritual of our days to check on the lamb every morning and feed him, even before we ate our own breakfasts. But one morning, we walked outside only to find the gate open and the lamb gone.

A horrible moan came from Nell, the first real sound we had heard from her. Then she began crying, a wail broken only by her halting gasps for air. Never before had I heard her cry or seen any signs of deep emotion.

Just then Jackson Stone walked out of the woods.

"You kids ain't looking for a lamb, I don't suppose?" he asked us with feigned innocence. "Well, I just saw one wandering into the woods. A little animal like that could get killed in woods like these," he added with what seemed a special relish.

"*You* let him out!" I shouted, ready to throw myself at him again in furious attack, whatever the consequences. But Jackson moved away, keeping his distance from us.

"I'm not saying that I did or didn't," he said. "There's nothing you could prove anyway."

"Forget him," Ben said. "Let us look for Nell's pet."

With that, we raced into the woods, little Nell trailing behind us. It might have been a half hour of thrashing through brush and forest before we found the lamb. The poor beast was barely able to stand. Its neck was stained with a great splash of its own red blood. Just then a dog began barking ferociously at us from a few feet away and slowly began advancing toward us. Ben looked straight into the eyes of the animal, whose lips were curled back to reveal a glistening set of pointed teeth. There was blood on its matted and soiled coat. I was startled to hear Ben, who had never taken his eyes off the dog, growl at the dog, who whined, spun around, and ran away.

Ben picked up the pitiable lamb and took him down to the clearing with the burnt circle. The fallen trees remained like the spokes of a wheel, radiating from the place I discovered when Ben first came to us. The place had a transforming effect on my brother. His eyes seemed to be focused far off into the distance as if he were imagining himself in another land, and he staggered toward the center hub of bare earth. As if he were in a trance, Ben placed the lamb on the ground and then gathered up dust and packed it into the animal's wounds. Then, cradling the animal — the two of them covered in dust and blood — Ben carried it back to its pen. But even before we returned, the animal began kicking and bleating with renewed energy, as if it had never been injured at all.

With the gate closed behind him, the lamb gamboled about his enclosure. Perhaps, I thought, the cuts had only been on the surface, more terrible in appearance than in reality.

Ben rummaged around for several pieces of metal, tied them together and hung them from the gate, so that anyone who opened it would set off an alarm.

Nell was transformed. She still did not speak but appeared to follow our conversations. She sat with us at meals and without any instruction learned to feed herself. It was as if she and the lamb, restored to health, were growing together.

I waited expectantly for Jackson Stone to strike back at us again, but weeks went by and I began to hope that he had forgotten all about us.

8

Miraculous Mud

One morning, a few days later, Ben and I were sent out to split up logs for kindling the wood stove.

It was already warm and the air was wet with the promise of a coming storm. The ax handle must have become wet with the sweat from Ben's hand, because it suddenly slipped from his grip. The blade cut deeply into his foot.

"Mama!" I cried as soon as I recognized the gravity of what had happened. But Ben, the injured one, kept his usual calm. He seemed more curious than in pain as I pulled the bloodied ax from his shoe. Charlotte, who could run as fast as I when she chose to, dashed from the house. Even she weakened at the sight of Ben's leather boot, split and oozing.

Mother joined us, taking charge, With her strong

arms, she carried Ben into the house and stretched him out on her own bed, the blood spilling out on the old but brightly colored patchwork quilt.

Ben pointed to his injured foot. "Is that blood?" he asked.

"Yes, it is," I said.

"Like the lamb?" he asked.

"Yes," I said. "Remember what happened to my nose . . ."

"When you walked into the tree?" Mother said.

"I, too, have blood," he said with a vague smile.

"Hush!" Mother said, as she loosened the ruined shoe and pulled it away from Ben's damaged foot. The shoe was filled with liquid.

"You'd better get Dr. Jensen," she instructed me. "Hurry!"

I hesitated, transfixed by the fearful sight of what once was Ben's whole foot.

"Hurry!" she reminded me. "I am depending on you."

But this once, after I had sprinted the whole way, there was no Dr. Jensen, just a message scribbled on a slate left leaning against his office door.

"At the Crispins," the note said. The Crispins' farm was perhaps four miles away, an hour's walk or more if you stopped to dangle your tired feet in a stream along the way.

I ran until my lungs ached, stopped to catch my breath, and then kept on running. Luckily, I spotted Dr. Jensen driving his carriage. He was already on his way home when I flagged him down, perhaps a mile and a half from the Crispins' place.

I doubt that the doctor's horse ever ran quite so quickly over that grooved country road. One day soon the roads would be properly graded and some paved, and the doctor would be able to retire his horse and make the journeys by automobile. But on that day, I sat beside him as we jounced along behind the sweating horse, and the doctor and I scarcely said a word to one another.

Halfway home, or was it more than halfway, he whispered something more to the air than to me — words that somehow chilled me.

"The Crispins too have found a child," he said.

"Like Ben and Nell?" I asked. My voice startled him, perhaps because he was so deep in thought that he had forgotten for a moment that I was there.

"Yes, like Ben and Nell. But not a hardy child at all. This boy, I am afraid, may not live so very long."

"Has the Crispins' boy learned to speak?"

"Not as well as Ben, but then he has been ill."

"Could he be a brother?" I asked. "A real brother to Nell and Ben, I mean."

"He could be," he said.

I sat for a time quietly wondering at the meaning of this new discovery and when the doctor had first known it.

"Won't their parents come to get them?" I asked, at last breaking the silence.

"That is possible. But if they abandoned their own children, or if the children were lost and a parent did not immediately seek them, then he will owe us an explanation."

When we arrived at our house, the doctor went straight to work without saying a word to Mother or to Charlotte, who whisked Nell out of the way.

Mother had tied a tourniquet around Ben's leg, just below the knee, and she had cleaned up the wound.

His foot was blue, and the jagged edge of the cut was pale, almost white.

Ben's face, too, was washed of color, but there was still a crazy smile on his lips. I could see no fear in his expression as he watched the activity about him, just a detached wonder at this piece of flesh, his foot, made meat.

"The cut goes to the bone," Dr. Jensen said. "I'm not sure we can save the foot, or how useful it would be if we did."

"Please, Charles, try," Mother said gravely.

The doctor went about his work almost soundlessly. As I watched, my admiration for him grew, and the event planted in me something that would bear fruit only much later and alter my own destiny.

He probed and cleaned the wound with carbolic acid, which filled the room with an antiseptic smell. Then he sewed the flesh back together, stitch upon tiny stitch. And all the while Ben sat quietly, without tears or cries or whimpers. "Good lad," the doctor said, as he completed his work.

The tourniquet removed, the foot became a vibrant red. The gash had become a seam, crossed by black threads as fine stitched as those that coursed through a quilt.

"We must watch for infection," the doctor said. "That's the main danger now."

I observed Dr. Jensen's appearance with a new and appreciative eye. He was tall and lean, the way I thought Abraham Lincoln must have been. His hair was lightly dusted with gray. His small, delicate hands could make knots as precise as any seamstress. I knew he was a bookish man. I had seen the volumes and the journals scattered over every available flat surface of his office, but here was evidence of his practical skill, the mending of bodies and the comforting of fears.

The bond between him and my mother had grown. At first, I was certain that I did not want him for a father. My dead father, unknown to me, had grown in my imaginings so that any living man must suffer in comparison. But now, watching the doctor repair Ben's torn foot, I suddenly found Dr. Jensen to be altogether admirable. And I welcomed a possibility that I had once feared: that he would become father to me, who had known no father.

With Mother's help, he carried Ben to the makeshift bed that Mother had given Ben in what had become our room. So narrow was the space that the two beds left only an awkward little aisle to walk through.

Ben was already asleep.

"Ah, stalwart Ben!" the doctor said and then sighed.

As my adopted brother turned in his sleep, Charlotte and Mother swept up the scraps of bandage and the nipped ends of suture and then swabbed down the floors.

While Ben slept on, we sat down to eat our evening meal in tired silence.

"The hardest part may be yet to come," Dr. Jensen finally said. "But there is nothing to do now but sleep on this afternoon's work and hope that the foot heals well."

When finally I, too, went off to bed, I fell into that deep, deep sleep that only the young seem to stumble into.

At the first light, I awoke with such a start to find that Ben was gone. A pile of dark, stained bandages lay on the floor.

Still in my nightshirt, I dashed outside and instinctively ran to the woods. The ground was wet and cool. On the same spot where I had found the burnt circle and the fallen trees, Ben sat with his bare, injured foot in one hand. He was packing his wound with the dirt and mud from the center of the circle.

"It is cool," he explained to me. "The mud stops the burning."

He rose to his feet and began to walk toward the house, but he was limping so badly that I ran up to him. As best I could with a boy my own size, I helped him back to the house. He radiated heat like a hot water bottle. By the time we reached the kitchen door, Mother came out to grab Ben from me, and I felt as if I had been responsible for taking him away.

When her cheek touched his forehead, she gasped, "He's burning up." And to me, she added, "Go get Dr. Jensen. Right away!"

And so fearful was I of pending calamity that I began to run.

"Stop!" Mother hollered. "I don't want the two of you sick. Get proper clothes and shoes on first, but hurry."

This time, Dr. Jensen was home. He did not stop to put his pony into harness. We ran together back to my house.

When we got there, Ben was crouched in a corner of the kitchen, growling like an animal — as if all the learning of the past few months since we had found him was forgotten and a more primitive spirit had once again taken hold.

"I tried to clean the mud from his foot, but he won't let me, Charles," Mother said to the doctor. She was tearful.

"He must be delirious," the doctor said. "Help me

hold him." With that, Dr. Jensen reached for the boy.

With a snap as sudden as a snake strike, Ben bit down on the doctor's hand.

"Damn the boy!" the doctor said.

I am not sure when Charlotte, still in her nightgown, entered the room, but her mere presence had a calming influence on Ben. She walked toward him fearlessly and surrounded him in her arms, just as she had done on that first day. The doctor, his courage renewed, moved toward the boy again, but this time more slowly. Ben growled ominously.

"Leave him alone!" Charlotte insisted. "He'll be fine now. He'll be fine."

The next few moments seemed to stretch out into hours. I looked around the room. All over the floor were trails of blood and mud, in broad strokes as if they had been painted on the planks with a large paintbrush. There were splatters on the yellow walls.

Mother turned her attention to Dr. Jensen, who seated himself by the table and asked me to bring him his bag. From it he took out a glass bottle, containing a thick red fluid more vivid and thick than blood itself. My mother swabbed the liquid over the doctor's wound and then, following his instructions, bandaged his hand.

The small surgical task might have been completed in two or three minutes, but in that time a remarkable transformation had overtaken Ben. His face, so taut and red just a minute or so before, had become slack and pink. He had sunk into Charlotte's arms and gone to sleep.

He offered no resistance as the doctor cleaned off the muddy foot and prepared some ointments to apply to it. Dr. Jensen paused to feel Ben's forehead.

"Thank God there is no fever," he said.

"He was burning up just a minute ago," Mother said, and she touched Ben's cheek and nodded. "Why, the fever is broken."

"And look at the boy's foot," the doctor said. "It appears to be healing already. I have never seen the like of this."

It was true. The edges of the jagged seam, criss-crossed with dark sutures, appeared to be joining together again, the line between them flat and fine.

"I don't think I will even need to bandage this, if the boy can keep it clean."

When Ben rose with Charlotte's help to his feet, awake now but still drowsy, he was able to walk without a limp. "I am sorry," Ben said to the doctor, who had quite forgotten about his own wound for the moment.

Mother gave us all a special breakfast of eggs and bacon and coffee with cream. As soon as the dishes were cleared away, the doctor left for home, but not before he went with me to the woods to the place where I had discovered those strange metallic fragments. It was there, from that burnt circle, that Ben had burst from out of the woods and into our lives. Dr. Jensen bent down and filled an empty jar with a generous sampling of earth.

It was only then that I noticed that Nell had been stalking behind us. She stood some distance away in a dense growth of trees, but I could see her small form, wearing a red dress that had once belonged to Charlotte. The doctor did not appear to see her, and I scuffed along behind him as he walked back toward the house. Suddenly, Nell charged toward the circle with uncharacteristic speed and began scooping up dirt, stuffing handfuls of it into her mouth. She was soon coated with dust and grime, and every part of her took on the color of earth except for the whites of her blinking eyes.

Dr. Jensen grabbed her and began pounding her on the back with a fist, until the little girl began coughing, spattering mud all over the three of us. He threw her over his shoulder and loped toward our house. "Elizabeth!" he called out. "E-liz-a-beth!"

Mother came running and met us in the middle of the meadow. When the doctor lowered Nell to the ground before him, the child seemed fine, save for the dirt that covered her. From her mouth came a strange gurgling, as if she were drowning, and then a sound that was instantly recognizable. "Mama!" The first word I heard from her lips, there it was again and unmistakable. "Mama!"

"Water," she said. "Water to drink."

Mother surrounded Nell in her arms and repeatedly kissed her, every movement daubing my mother with that miraculous mud. Nell gained the full power of speech slowly over the many weeks that followed. Unlike Ben, she was not particularly talkative or inquisitive, but a new intelligence radiated from her large eyes. And by November, after harvesttime, she was ready to begin school with the rest of us.

By then Ben's wound had healed completely, his foot bore only the faintest of scars. Naturally enough, I was certain that the mud, and the mud alone, was responsible for Nell's transformation and the healing of Ben's wound. Just as I had seen Dr. Jensen dig up dirt from the burnt circle, I, too, collected some into a jar and began to experiment with my own scrapes and scratches. But I quickly discovered that the mud did nothing for these minor injuries except to make them dirty and earn me a scolding from Mother, who scoffed at my claim that the mud was somehow magic.

One afternoon I even suggested to Dr. Jensen that he try some of the mud on the bite that Ben had given him, which was still bandaged several weeks later.

"I have already tried your remedy, Roger," the doctor said, unwrapping his hand so that I might see the results of his experiment. His finger remained swollen and oozing. "Human bites are slow to heal and can prove extremely dangerous," he explained. "I believe my hand to be mending, but as you can see, an application of mud from the sample I took has not proved to be medicinal."

Ben seemed puzzled when I asked him about it. "There is healing in the mud," he insisted.

"But why won't it work when Dr. Jensen or I try it?" I asked.

"Part of the healing is here," he said, holding up his hands and gazing at them. "It is a gift given to me."

"Won't you show me how?" I said.

"I cannot because I do not understand."

And when I gave him severed earthworms to mend or a jay bird with a broken leg, he refused to demonstrate his powers. "I can do it only when it is needed," he said.

"Needed for what?" I asked.

He seemed to be trying very hard to find the words for a proper explanation. "I . . . I . . . cannot say," he finally spluttered. "I cannot say."

9

An Education

The school was a very old one, with a single room and a lone teacher, the wife of Peter Winfield. He was the railroad clerk, who kept the schedules, recorded the shipments, and sold tickets at the little station house in our town. Mrs. Winfield was everything that her husband was not: he was pale and pointed; she was red and round. He was almost always silent, and insulting when he was not; she was loud and lavishly generous of praise. He made his marks in his ledgers in a small, crimped hand; she scribbled across the chalkboard, the letters free and full.

Her name was Annabella Rose Winfield, a name that could be written, as she often did, on the board with a great flourish, a name that in all of its length and variety was an exercise in penmanship all by itself.

We went early to school that first day to introduce our foundling brother and sister. Mrs. Winfield greeted us in the cloakroom.

"There's my little Roger and, oh, Charlotte, how you have grown in just a summer," she said. "And I can see that you have brought some new children with you."

By then, certainly, everyone in town knew the history of Ben and of Nell as well. And yet Mrs. Winfield acted as if their arrival at school on that morning was a complete surprise.

"What would your names be?" she asked them.

"Benjamin," he said.

"And my name is Nell."

"And you have no surname to go with it?"

"Westwood, same as ours," I offered.

"I want to hear *them* say it," the teacher said.

"Benjamin Westwood."

"Both Westwoods, are you?" Mrs. Winfield asked.

"Mama says that we will soon be able to adopt them," Charlotte explained.

"Let us see if you can write your own name, Mr. Benjamin Westwood," Mrs. Winfield said cheerfully.

"I doubt they can," I interjected, trying to save them embarrassment.

"Let us show them then," the teacher said, writing out Ben's name on a large board and then handing him a small slate to copy it on. I watched Ben's dazzled eyes following the great curved trails left by Mrs. Winfield's chalk.

"He has never written anything before," I said protectively.

Ben ignored me, closing his eyes and letting his hand

glide across the slate without any apparent guidance from his head and eyes. He held it up for Mrs. Winfield, who snatched the slate from him and then turned it for Charlotte and me to see. "Benjamin Westwood," it said.

"The penmanship is quite as fine as my own," said a pleasantly surprised Mrs. Winfield. "It could serve as an example to you both," she added to Charlotte and me.

"And you, little Nell, let us see what you can do."

Nell, who had never until a few weeks before even spoken a word, took the slate and scratched out two words upon it. The teacher took up the board, but instead of being impressed, she laughed.

"Your handwriting too is quite splendid," the teacher said, "but I trust that your name is not the same as your brother's."

In a hand that mimicked Mrs. Winfield's, Nell had written the words "Benjamin Westwood" on the slate-board.

The teacher was so pleased with her two new charges that she let them ring the school bell that brought in the other children.

Will Crispin, arriving last of all, sat down on the same bench with Ben and me. "We found one, too," he said a little breathlessly as he stared at Ben. "But ours died."

I wanted to hear more about the Crispins' child, but Mrs. Winfield looked sourly at Will and cut off any hope that I might satisfy my curiosity before the morning recess.

I wondered how Ben and Nell had so quickly mastered penmanship of a quality that I could not duplicate myself. And all that first day, they continued to surprise, first with what they did not know, and then with what they could so quickly master.

"Read this for me, Ben," Mrs. Winfield commanded as she handed him the reading book that I had begun my own reading in just a few years before.

"But I cannot read," he said.

"Then you must listen as Roger reads," she said, handing me the well-worn book. I read him three brief pages.

"Now read them back, Benjamin," Mrs. Winfield ordered.

Hardly glancing at the pages, Ben faultlessly repeated every word and then stopped.

"Go on," she commanded.

He closed his eyes for a moment and then began reading very fast through the next several pages. He seemed not to be following the lines word by word. Instead, he took in whole pages with a glance.

"Why, you are a fine reader, Ben," the teacher said. "And you will do well not to hide your light under a bushel in the future."

"What do you mean about a bushel?" Ben asked, genuinely puzzled and seeming in that moment to be the hopeless moron that his reading ability belied.

"It is a saying," Mrs. Winfield cheerily explained. "It means that you should not hide your knowledge, but should let it shine brightly. You should have told me that you did know how to read."

"This is the first time for me," Ben said.

"You will soon get used to school," she said, certain that he could not mean that he had never before read from a book in his life. "Your parents must have taught you very well indeed," she added, turning away to address the whole class before Ben could dispute her remark.

At recess, Ben tagged behind me and Will Crispin as we went outside to a clear and windy day.

A strong hint of winter was in the air. Although it was autumn still, few trees retained their leaves, and the ground was only now beginning to thaw from the night's cold breath.

"I'm not supposed to tell," said Will, who then eagerly spilled out his secrets.

"We were all in the fields, even Mama, cultivating the squash. Mama and I left for the house early, before dark, so she could cook supper, and we found this boy, stripped naked and squatting down on the porch like he owned it and nobody could step up there without being attacked. He growled fearsomely, but Mama wasn't afraid. She covered him and took him into the house and fed him, and we kept him like he was our own.

"But he took ill and he died. Dr. Jensen said he had some parts missing. I am not sure what. He looked the same as you and me."

"Did he look like Ben?" I asked.

"No, he wasn't dark like you and Ben. He was fair," Will said. "And he wasn't full-sized like Ben is. More about my size, or smaller. I don't know if he would have gone to school even if he hadn't died. I'm not supposed to say anything about him. Mama said it would mean a whipping if any of us told. She thinks people will think it's her fault that the boy never got well. But Papa says that's silly and that no one could deny we gave him the very best of care, which Dr. Jensen agrees to."

I tried to drag more out of Will. Had the boy been buried? And, if so, where? What had been the matter with him? Did he have a fever? Before he died, did he ever learn to speak like Ben?

But Will bit down on his lower lip, as if he could only keep the words in by locking his teeth on a flap of flesh and holding on tight.

Just then, Jackson Stone, who had crept up behind us, grabbed Will by the ear and pulled him from us.

"You can tell me all about it," the large boy said. As much of a terror as Jackson had been during the summer months, he seemed even more of a bully during the school year, when his unhappiness and cruelty toward others only increased.

"I have nothing to tell *you*, Jackson Stone," little Will said gamely.

"You just leave Will alone," Ben said flatly, with no hint that he was either angry or frightened.

I thought there would be another bloody confrontation and I felt my muscles tensing, ready to throw myself into a struggle. But I was not so sure that the outcome would be to my own liking this time. Ben seemed fragile when head to head with Jackson.

The bell sounded to end the recess. The three of us smaller boys scurried back to class, but Jackson skulked away and did not return to school again for a full three days. When he came back, he said that he had been sick. But I wondered if in truth he was afraid that Ben would beat him again, this time in front of the entire school.

In class that first day, and again and again in the days that followed, Ben and Nell showed that, far from being imbeciles, they both had remarkable minds. Ben, for example, could recite long lists of spelling words, their definitions, and sentences showing how to use them as effortlessly as most of us could rattle off what we liked to eat for dinner.

They both seemed to have a photographic memory: whatever they glanced at, they retained in their brains as perfectly as if it all were placed on film and then neatly filed away.

But for many, many months, there continued to be yawning gaps in their knowledge — so much so that as brilliant as they might seem one second, they could seem thoroughly feebleminded the next.

Nell knew nothing of the seasons. The idea that the pond would freeze solid in the next few months, permitting us to skate across its surface, was a complete surprise to her. She wondered how we would allow the world to become so cold in order to enjoy such a simple pleasure. As if we had any control over winter!

When Mrs. Winfield told her that in the spring the bare trees and bushes would grow green and bloom once more, Nell was terribly perplexed.

"How can you be certain that the leaves will come again?" she asked.

"Because they always have, Nell," the teacher said. "It is the wisdom of Nature that plants must lose their leaves in one season and then regain them in the next."

"But what has always been, may not always be," Ben boldly chimed in. We all laughed an uproarious, superior laugh. We knew nothing of ice ages that might again reach with glacial fingers around the globe. We had no science books to tell us that millions upon millions of years hence, the sun itself would lose its energy and grow cold. None of us knew that there would be weapons in great numbers that could still the creatures of the earth and truly end the seasons.

Perhaps Ben and Nell in their innocence knew more about the uncertain nature of things than we did.

Ben, who was the more talkative of the two, was always surprising us. He had trouble believing that bears and newts and insects might hibernate but that humans could not.

"It would be handy to learn how," Ben said.

And he was baffled when other children talked of leaving the earth in rockets to travel to the moon, an idea that was the stuff of cheap novels.

"Is the moon not a lifeless stone?" he asked.

Nothing mystified him as much as war, however.

"You say that men destroy other men and even risk their own lives to do so? And they act thus willingly?" Ben asked Mrs. Winfield.

"We do not want that to happen, ever," said Mrs. Winfield, who adopted a certain exasperated tone whenever Ben appeared to be so ignorant of the ways of the world.

"But men who are good at killing other men are heroes," he said. "Some we have made Presidents."

"Yes," said the teacher, smiling with the rest of the class. "Men like George Washington did not like war. They acted out of principle. That is why they are heroes."

"Is it not one of our first principles that men should not kill other men?"

"Oh, Ben," said the teacher. "I wish the world were quite that simple."

Like the rest of us, Ben soon learned to speak well of Washington, even though he had commanded an army, and of Abraham Lincoln, although he had forced young men to war. He learned to view the fighting of the American Revolution and the slaughter of the Civil War just as we did, as necessary even if the reasons for them were not always so simple to explain.

At just that time, in distant lands, there was talk of war again. Soon enough, nations all about the globe would be clashing with other nations. And little boys playing with toy rifles would wish that they could join the battle.

10

A Change of Fortune

After school and on weekends, the boys of our town liked to play at war. Many of us had fashioned weapons from old broom handles and other scraps. Some were able to make their rifles look as convincingly real as the toy guns that are sold in stores today.

When Ben joined us in our games, he seemed as enthusiastic as the rest of us, I thought. But though he would point his rifle at the rival army, I noticed that he never pretended to be shooting it.

"You could have killed all five of them," I once said to him, as we peered down the hill at the other side's advancing troops.

"I would never hurt your kind," he said.

I was puzzled. "But it is just a game," I said.

"The games we play are real enough to me," he responded.

He was so quick of mind, so agile of body, that Ben should have been our natural leader. But he refused that role. He seemed to love to take orders from the older boys, who liked to line us up in a row and have us march along in lines as straight as the British soldiers formed during the Revolutionary War.

His sense of order, of what was proper, was annoying. As long as what he was ordered to do seemed fair, he would do it almost cheerfully. He was obedient to a fault. And among us children, he gained a reputation as someone who refused to speak up for himself, as a kind of coward.

Only the few of us who had seen him stand up to Jackson Stone knew that he was not a coward at all. But those of us who knew better were still perplexed by his generally docile behavior.

Adults, too, began to find him a strange boy, even eerie.

"He is such a *good* boy," I heard Mother tell Charlotte that winter. "But I do wish that he would be *just* a boy once in a moon. Sometimes I think he has no gumption at all."

"He can be strong," Charlotte said, her face flushing with anger. "When he needs to, he can stand up for himself and others."

So it was that within a few months of starting school, my brother Ben was resented by most of our schoolmates. And even the growing evidence of his extraordinary intelligence had not won him the approval of the adults we knew. Maybe in that particular place and time, intelligence was regarded as less a virtue than the more ordinary ones of pluck and the courage it takes to contradict an elder.

Ben surely knew that he was not liked by other children, although he struggled not to show it. He began having nightmares, very loud ones at that. His shouting would wake me in the middle of the night. Time and again, I would awake with a start to his delirious babbling. I tried to make some sense from the strange speech that poured from him, but I was so sleepy that I could not seem to understand a word, or, if I did, remember what he said until morning.

For weeks, I plotted almost daily to keep myself awake all night so that I would be alert enough to understand him during one of these episodes.

My scheme usually failed because I simply could not keep myself awake long enough to reach the dead of night when Ben's babble seemed always to begin.

But one November morning, well before dawn, he had one of those terrible dreams, and I clearly made out one of the words that he kept repeating. "Monster," he said. "Monster." Then he flung himself up with a snap as fast as a mousetrap. His eyes were open wide and he pointed a long finger at me and shouted again, "Monster."

It took both Mother and Charlotte to quiet him down again. And that night, I think that none of us was able to get back to sleep.

For the entire day that followed, Ben kept unusually quiet, even fearful. I did not know why.

He acted as if he were afraid of us. Whenever anyone came close, he became as vigilant as a bird picking seeds from a garden. Only Nell, small and soft-spoken, could creep up beside Ben without startling him.

But one Saturday afternoon in midwinter, Ben's mood

and fortunes shifted. The snow was falling in large, wet clumps ideal for packing into treacherous snowballs. And every boy in town was in our meadow, stockpiling them in preparation for a battle.

Ben and I, along with a few of the other smaller boys, built a barricade in front of a shed not far from our house. Another bunch of larger boys had grouped behind a fence perhaps 20 yards away.

At an arbitrary moment, when a boy in our group could hold himself back no longer, the battle began. It proved to be a vicious one. Almost at the very start, a hard, wet snowball hit me squarely in the face, so hard that I might have even blacked out for a minute.

I saw Ben through my tears, smiling at me with that idiotic grin of his. "Blood," he said, now very familiar with the liquid that was spurting again from my long and delicate nose. I had no time to assess the damage, only enough to wipe my face off on the sleeve of my coat and try to keep the other boys from advancing on our barrier as they continued to pummel us.

Suddenly we began to feel a hail of missiles dropping down on us from behind. One of the boys had climbed up on the shed and was peppering us from above with dangerously hard snowballs.

It was Jackson Stone, who was singling me out for his wrath. I could see him grinning down on us, when I was not blinking or hiding my face behind an arm. It was as if he thought that the best way to hurt Ben was to hurt someone who was closest to him.

But just as suddenly as the fight had begun, it ended. Jackson lost his footing, skidded off the low roof, and bounced off a wood pile and onto the snowy ground. A hush fell over the battlefield as we all waited to see if he could move. At first he did not stir at all, not a breath could be heard. Then he let out a howl that any one of us would surely be ashamed of. But when we saw the wound, we all understood. A gleaming object, white and red, protruded from a tear in his pant leg.

"He's broken his leg!" someone shouted.

A guilty panic ensued, with boys running in every direction, fleeing from any connection to this horrid injury. Only Ben seemed undisturbed, almost unnaturally calm and, for once, in command.

"Get Mama," he said to me. And then he bent low over Jackson's twitching body and pulled the large boy's leg straight. In a matter of seconds, he fashioned a splint from belts and the branches we pulled out of the woodpile. By that time I was running for home. I turned to look back once and saw Ben pick up Jackson as easily as the muscled clerk in the general store might pick up a sack of flour.

Putting the boy over his shoulder, Ben carried him to our house, a distance of a quarter of a mile. By chance, Dr. Jensen had stopped by on a visit, and he tried to help Ben as he stretched Jackson across Mother's bed.

"Why, that boy is five years your senior, Ben," Dr. Jensen said. "And he is twice your weight."

For all of his size, Jackson at that moment seemed frail enough. He said nothing, but closed his eyes when Dr. Jensen examined him.

"Perfectly placed and splinted," the doctor said after he had carefully snipped the clothing from the injured boy's leg. "Have you ever seen a splint placed before, Ben? Why, surely you have!"

Ben said nothing. He seemed as tired as Jackson, gravely tired, as if his exertion had left him run down, as if a wind-up mechanism inside of him had spent all of its force.

Dr. Jensen took Jackson home. The boy recovered quickly, without even a limp to show for his injury.

But Ben's fatigue seemed to last for months. The long period of poor health that plagued him after the rescue was the first definite warning of what was to become a common pattern in Ben's life. He had at times almost supernatural powers, but after those times he would lapse into supernatural weakness.

As the seasons turned and spring finally arrived, the two of us were able to run through the woods again. And Jackson, long ago completely mended, would drop by, mostly to sit on the sidelines as we played our still childish games. But he never scoffed at us. Instead, he watched us protectively. He remained a fearsome boy, one who often got into fights over minor or nonexistent insults. But he saw to it that no one ever bullied Ben or me again.

Ben's progress in school continued at an astonishing pace. He soon left everyone else behind, including the oldest of the children. One evening Dr. Jensen suggested to Mother that Ben ought to be sent off to a boarding school, one of the many fine ones near Boston.

"We could never afford it," she said. "And he is such a little boy to be away from home, even if we could."

"Then let me tutor him instead," the doctor said. "I will take on all four of them. Roger and Charlotte and Nell could benefit as well."

Mother agreed.

Although Ben's brilliance dimmed my own achievements, I, too, excelled in school, as did Charlotte.

Nell preferred to keep silent; she shrank away from asking questions. But during Mrs. Winfield's lessons, I could see that she paid very close attention. When called on, she always knew the answer.

Dr. Jensen began working with the four of us at the kitchen table, the room illuminated by kerosene lanterns. The fluttering fire shone through the grating of the wood stove, which Mother tended for us in the cool springtime evenings.

Later in the evenings, after we children had gone off to bed, we could hear Dr. Jensen's deep voice resounding through our house, its resonance picked up by the rafters and the frame of the building. That rumbling voice of his became a backdrop to my falling asleep. It accompanied my dreams, just as the sound of a stream or the whisper of wind through the trees is background to walking through the woods.

As the days became longer and warmer, and the brooks and pond swelled with the melted snow from the shoulders of the hills and mountains — with that same certainty of season — Mother and Dr. Jensen announced that they were going to be wed.

11

A Gathering of the Clan

Hundreds of people came to the wedding. Some came because they knew my mother, but a far larger number were there because of Dr. Jensen, the only doctor for miles around. He was greatly respected, even though people thought it a little stange to see a man, even a doctor, so soft and bookish in a world that required sinew and toil.

Doctors in those days were not necessarily wealthy men or even well-to-do. If they depended solely on their labors for a living, they were no richer than the patients they served. But by the standards of our town, Dr. Jensen was prosperous. He had property — a large house, a horse and carriage, and his beloved collection of books. On this occasion he wore a dark new suit, complete with vest, much like the town banker's.

Ben and I also sported new clothes that Dr. Jensen purchased for us. They were the first suits we had ever owned, identical in cut and cloth but not in length. Ben, who had been close enough in size to be my twin, was now two or three inches taller. The change had come about so gradually that I did not give it a thought until Mother remarked about the difference in tailoring. Still, many of the guests remarked that we looked alike enough to be natural brothers if not twins. That observation embarrassed me, but gave Ben considerable pleasure and he beamed every time it was pronounced.

The new clothes made me uncomfortable. The itchy wool pants and jacket were warm, especially so as we chased through the crowd and in and out of the house. We squirmed from the unaccustomed feel of tight collars and bow ties that felt like choking hands about our necks.

Charlotte and Nell, too, had new clothes for the occasion, store-bought dresses that Dr. Jensen and Mama had helped them choose. Charlotte was on the brink of womanhood, although just a few years older than the two of us boys. I found myself marveling at her appearance in that long checked dress with ruffled lace around the sleeves, the neck, and the hem. I can see her still as she was then. To my surprise, she seemed truly beautiful. Ben noticed her, too, and many times that day, as we helped prepare for the great celebration and then later in the midst of it, I caught him gazing at her.

I caught myself looking at Nell in her long, grown-up gown. I could not help remembering how she was when we first saw her, smaller and thinner, and covered in the grime of the county home.

Mrs. Dublin, the woman we knew as Nell's mother, was among the first guests to arrive. The old woman caught me with one claw, and waving a perfumed handkerchief with the other, she proclaimed: "You have completely transformed the girl! If Dr. Jensen and your mother had not come along when they did, I am not sure what would have become of her."

Nell shrank from the old woman, and when commanded to kiss her, took Mrs. Dublin's hand and bowed down to kiss it, as if she were a Victorian gentleman greeting a lady.

Here, too, was Jackson Stone, in a worn brown jacket a size or two too small for him. The tight clothing made him seem even larger and more formidable. He was now almost a man, but he shyly kept his distance from the rest of us until Charlotte coaxed him to join us.

The bride and groom and as many guests as could fit stood at last under a broad canopy that Dr. Jensen had pitched in the meadow. Not everyone was able to crowd into the shade that it cast. But Nell was there with a bouquet of flowers and Charlotte with another. Mother had grown the blooms herself in a doorway garden.

Because of the high excitement of the day, I remember only a few details. I keep with me an impression of brilliant light all about the shaded wedding party. It was the reverse of a theater, where the stage and actors are bathed in light and the audience in the dark. Here the main actors stood in the cool shade, and the surrounding company, as well as the trees, the house, the garden patch, were flooded in light.

I found myself glancing again at Nell, who stood unhappily by Mrs. Dublin, but looked at me from time to time with darkest eyes and smiled.

A party followed. Salted meats and salads and peas, breads and cakes and fruits were spread out on long tables in the shade of the house. With the turn of a spigot, frothy beer flowed into waiting glasses. For the children, there was a deep red punch, more vibrantly colored than any ordinary juice or wine, and syrupy in its sweetness.

A lone fiddler — another of Dr. Jensen's patients — played dance tunes, and all the children began to dance and clap, even me, after a bit of teasing from Charlotte. The adults all turned to watch us, a ring of dancing children that included even Jackson Stone. We danced for hours, the adults joining in as evening came, when the first stars shone down from the dusky sky.

I left the dancing for a minute to get more punch and another piece of cake or slice of pie. When I returned I found Ben and Nell on the edge of the dancing, standing together, their eyes fixed on a distant, unblinking star.

"It is so beautiful," she said, and I did not know whether she was talking about the wedding, the party, or the emerging night sky. I wanted to tell her that she, too, was beautiful, but I could not manage it. She seemed to read my thoughts, because she turned and kissed me. Her lips felt cool to my cheek, but I could feel a warm blush spread across my face and a burning in my ears. Before I could think of what to say, she ran away. I need not have been embarrassed. Ben seemed to pay no attention, and the two of us walked back to the party silently until we found the other children.

When the moon rose, looking like a silver coin against a black cloth of sky, the guests began to leave. We four children joined Mother and Dr. Jensen in a line as the others bid the newlyweds best wishes and goodnight. I was tired and scarcely paying attention to the many kindnesses expressed until it was the turn of a man and woman I had never seen before this day.

"You have done considerable good with these children," the woman said to Mother and Dr. Jensen. "I just wish *our* boy might have done so well, poor thing."

"We all did what we could to save him, Mrs. Blyleven, you and your husband most of all," the doctor said.

"I never did expect much," the woman said. "He was sickly the moment we found him, picking for something to eat out of our compost."

"It was a night like this when we saw him," explained the man by her side, her husband, Mr. Blyleven. "Only there were more shooting stars than anyone would care to count that night. And then to find a wild thing sifting through the garbage, and to find that he is a boy, and sick for so, so long and then to pass on.

"But that is enough morbid thinking for tonight," Mr. Blyleven added, forcing himself to become cheerful. "Tonight we celebrate the living, doctor and bride, and you have our heartiest congratulations, you and your fine family."

As they walked away and to their wagon, I grabbed Dr. Jensen by a loose sleeve. "That makes *four* of them," I said. "Their boy, the Crispins', Nell, and Ben."

"It is strange to believe," the doctor said softly.

It had been a very long day, and I did not press him further. We New Englanders are a taciturn people, and we guard our thoughts as closely as we guard our fortunes, perhaps more so. When he was ready to explain, if ever, he would do so.

The doctor extended a long arm to Mother, who draped it about her shoulders. We all walked back to the house.

"I hope you children can come to think of me as a father," the doctor said.

In many ways, although we did not say it to him that night, we already did.

12

Discoveries

The newly wedded couple had no time for a honeymoon. Instead, with the help of several townspeople, we spent the next several days moving our belongings to Dr. Jensen's house. At first, our new home seemed so large that I was sure I would always feel lost in it. Although it was in many ways a modest house, it seemed a mansion to me. It had many more rooms than Mother's house, including an office for seeing patients and a combination library and laboratory. There were three rooms that Dr. Jensen did not appear to use at all; they were empty except for dust and cobwebs.

Ben and I chose to share the attic, although we could each have had rooms of our own on the second floor, where Nell and Charlotte decided to share one.

Our attic was large and open, broken up here and there by wood columns that supported the roof. Mother hung old sheets from post to post to break up the space into separate areas. A small door opened out to the house's lower roof.

On a warm summer evening, we would crouch low on the slanting shingles and watch the bats appear in the final blaze of sun as it set over the forested hills. Ben could stay on to watch the stars for hours, long after I lost interest. Dr. Jensen — or Father as we all promised to call him — gave Ben a book of constellations that charted the movement of the stars across the sky.

"The ancient Greeks watched these same constellations parade across the night, season after season," Father told us. "But there are still new wonders to be found out there for those who choose to search for them."

After he had gone, leaving us the task of identifying the star formations he told us to look for, Ben pointed to a bright star in the middle of the sky.

"Father calls it Vega," he said. "But to me, it is the guide star."

"What is a guide star?" I asked.

"I do not know why I have given it such a name," he said, seemingly as baffled by his own words as I was. "I see it in a dream that I keep having. In the dream, I am standing in a crowd and then suddenly I am unable to move, not even to breathe. Soon I am far above the earth, cold and afraid. But there above me in the night sky is a bright star, one of the brightest in the heavens. And I say to myself, 'There is the guide star. It will lead me home.' "

"But this is your home," I said, fearful at the sudden

76

idea that he might find a way to leave the earth and travel to the heavens.

"Perhaps it was the guide star that led me here," he said. "I know no way of getting there," he laughed, looking at the sky. The stars were a part of his innermost life, even of his dreams. He already wanted to spend the rest of his life studying them.

But I preferred Father's medical books. And with some effort, I learned the names of all the bones, muscles, nerves, and arteries.

One summer afternoon, when no patients were expected to call, Father showed Charlotte, Ben, and me how to prepare frogs for dissection. Nell, when asked if she wanted to watch, shook her head and ran away. The three of us had collected the specimens by the pond, where they seemed to grow from the muddy shore. They were proud, fat little creatures that were difficult to hold onto. We were to copy Father as he plunged a wire through the animal's skull and into its brain. And just as Father showed us, we were to expose the delicate inner anatomy of the debrained animals, using his collection of picks and pins and scalpels. Inside, he told us, we would even see the beauty of the beating heart.

Ben balked even before the first step. Unwilling to scramble and destroy the animals' brains, he begged Father to release them.

At first, Father insisted that Ben go ahead. "To be a truly educated man, Ben, you must learn science," he said. "And to know science, you must learn anatomy. A man of science has an obligation to study nature in all of its variety. He must put squeamishness aside."

Suddenly I remembered to be squeamish myself as

77

I looked down at my glistening specimen, which would leap away if it could, its inner secrets all intact.

Charlotte did not let the argument slow her. She plunged ahead. With its brain destroyed, her frog gave a little reflex hop or two and then lay still.

"It is no different than killing a chicken or slaughtering a pig," Charlotte said.

"You do not object to our slaughtering an animal for its meat," Father joined in.

"We must eat to live," Ben said.

"But for mankind, to know is also to live," Father replied.

"There are other ways of knowing," Ben said solemnly.

"Come, Ben. How could we know the inner workings of an animal without looking inside?" Father asked.

"By observing the outside," Ben said. "If we watch closely, we can know what is within by seeing how it reacts and behaves."

"But that fear of exploring beneath the surface led to centuries of error that we are only now beginning to dispel," Father retorted.

"The past error does not make it right to do what is wrong, as long as there are other ways of knowing," Ben said.

Father and Ben stood face to face. I realized then that my brother was already fast approaching the height of an adult. In many ways he had become more manly than I, and even had a faint but unmistakable growth of hair on his upper lip. At the same time, Father and Mother treated him with a kind of deference that was not shown to the other children. It seemed altogether proper that Ben should challenge Father. But I would not have done so for fear that I might anger him.

"I will do as you say only because you have asked me to do it," Ben said.

"Then you need not do it at all," Father said with finality.

Ben left the rest of us to our dissection, taking his frog with him. I supposed that he planned to return it to the pond.

It was that afternoon that our educations began to diverge. Father, Charlotte, and I worked together to explore the biological sciences. With Ben, Father explored the heavens, where the objects were too large and too remote to be dissected. Instead, they had to be watched, to see their reactions to other objects, to chart their behavior by observation so that their inner workings could be understood.

Nell often ran away from Father's lessons or kept her distance and watched us quietly.

The four of us children spent much time together. We all worked in Mother's garden, where Ben proposed a series of plant experiments. He believed there was a way to select faster-growing tomatoes as well as those that grew more slowly, so that we would have them over a longer season. But it was I who produced the largest cucumber; and Charlotte the longest carrot; and Nell the biggest crop of green beans.

Hot from our work, we often scurried up to the pond for a swim and to explore the surrounding wood. Late in the season, the pond became muddy and was not as pleasant to swim in as it was earlier in the summer. But Charlotte and I knew of a cool cave on the distant shore where we could find some relief from the sun's relentless heat. The two of us showed Nell and Ben the way.

The pond lapped up to the cave's entrance, and we

waded through a shallow stretch of water to enter. Nell began crying as the water deepened, but I took her hand and led her in. Inside I immediately sniffed at a sour smell in the air, like the odor of early spring when the snow has just melted and the earth is rank with thawed decay.

I lit a candle. In the faint light, we could see a large object floating in the water. I felt a bit panicky when I recognized a cylinder of coiled gray metal — a haunting reminder of the object I had seen floating on the pond on the day of Ben's arrival.

"Don't touch it!" I shouted. "Let's get Father!"

We raced down to the house to find him. Charlotte and I ran at full speed, Charlotte ahead of me. But Ben gave up running and walked down the path, pulling Nell along and falling far behind.

We had to wait for several minutes until Father was finished seeing a patient. I found myself looking up toward the path, half expecting to see a wild creature burst from the woods and run to our house. Father made us wait until he could gather some equipment together, a lantern, a cloth sack, and some medical tools.

When we neared the cave, Father lit the lantern and holding it high in the air followed me in. When he saw the object in the water, he handed me the lantern and with the utmost caution touched the cylinder. Its shell cracked open. Inside was a pale, soft creature with large, fishlike eyes. It was identical to the one I had seen floating in the pond so many months before.

Nell began to whimper, like a frightened puppy, and Ben led her out of the cave.

"It's like a large embryo!" Father exclaimed. "It is

unlike anything I have seen or heard of on this earth!"

Father unrolled the cloth sack and tried to slip the creature into it, but it was too large. He took off his jacket and used it as a sling to hold it as he staggered out of the cave. It was a clumsy load, but he managed to carry it all the way back to the house without dropping it.

Charlotte and I ran ahead, chattering about our discovery and anxious to tell Mother about it. We were wildly excited, the way explorers must have been when they first encountered the mummies of the pharaohs. When they caught up with us, however, Ben and Nell remained strangely quiet, even sad, as if the event were somber as a funeral.

Father placed the thing on an examining table. In the full light that shone through the windows of his office, the creature did not seem quite so terrible. It was like a small child, but much more rounded — puffy really, as if it were made of bread dough that had been allowed to rise a bit in a warm kitchen.

Mother came in and seemed more alarmed at Father's appearance than at the creature. He was wet and muddy and all over him were flecks of metallic gray.

That afternoon, Father dissected the creature. I assisted him, mostly by fetching jars and sorting through his cutting tools. From time to time as Father worked, he stopped to write notes into a laboratory book. Often he would try to explain to me what he was finding in that curiously bloodless flesh, but I understood little of what he told me.

I was much impressed with the way he dropped pieces of the creature into jars that he had filled with a liquid that gave off such a rich, sweet odor that I can still bring it to mind as I write. At the thought of that smell, something deep inside my brain brings back the whole of that warm afternoon, when the fumes were real and only my excitement kept me from swooning.

Charlotte had left with Mother before the dissection had begun. Nell and Ben had disappeared. Nell turned up a few hours later, looking particularly gaunt and pale.

Ben did not return until well after dinner. When he did arrive, I was banished from the room while Mother questioned him. From the hall outside the room I could hear only bits and pieces of conversation.

"I am not a monster," Ben said in a loud and plaintive voice.

"Of course, you are not," Mother said. From his muffled sobs, I knew that Mother had pulled him close to her to ease his distress.

In the weeks that followed, Father kept the sealed jars on the shelves that lined his library. At least twice, he sent off samples to distant places in what I thought was an effort to convince others of an important discovery. The remaining dissected parts floated in their clear containers. From one of them an eye stared out into the room and seemed to follow me wherever I moved, so that even I found it difficult to stay in that room. Ben refused to go into the room at all, unless he had to. And then he would gaze anywhere but at those clear glass jars.

Father finally removed them, packing them together with his notebooks into a large wood crate that remained in his study for many days and one day vanished, never to reappear.

13

Unwelcome Changes

We all returned to school again, to the one-room schoolhouse of Mrs. Winfield and to evenings by lantern's light with Father. Season followed season, as if to prove to Nell and to Ben that the earth was indeed reliable. In February, after a heavy snow, Ben and I together celebrated my twelfth birthday, since we did not know his. It was difficult to remember that we were both the same size when we found him, because he was long and wiry and he towered above me. I suppose I was small for my age; even Nell was a little taller. In March, Charlotte turned 16, which was cause for a party. Father brought out a bottle of sparkling cider from the cellar, and I felt tipsy as I danced with Charlotte and then with Nell around our kitchen floor.

"It will be so hard to see you leave," Nell said.

"And just where is it that I am going?" I said, still dizzy from our dancing.

"Oh, then he has not told you," she said, her face flushing. Then she looked to Father. "I am very sorry, I thought that he must know."

Father too seemed embarrassed. "I have found a school for you and Ben," he said.

"But we have a school already."

"And it is very good, for a country school," Father said. "But both you boys have outgrown what Mrs. Winfield can teach you. And I do not have the time to give you all that your intelligence requires."

"And what about Charlotte and Nell?" I said. "Will they be going, too?"

"No, I have not found a suitable school for them, but I have found one of the very best for you and Ben. I plan to take you boys there for a visit in a few weeks. You will be able to see it for yourself."

It did not seem fair to me that Ben and I should have to go when Charlotte and Nell did not. Yet on a chilly spring morning, when winter had not yet loosened its hold on the earth, he took the two of us by train to visit the school.

Hill in the Forest School was a cluster of red brick buildings, their walls crusted with brown branches of ivy that had not yet begun leafing out. Here and there in the woods around the school were still patches of grimy snow.

I still wore the suit from the wedding, but Ben had long before outgrown his. Mother had helped him pick out a new one, choosing one a little too large for him so that he might grow into it. We must have been a remarkable sight, the two of us, in our ill-fitting clothes, looking like country folk. Perhaps that was why the schoolboys who passed us all seemed to be either laughing or sneering at us, as we wandered the grounds looking for the headmaster's cottage.

When we finally arrived and were seated in the headmaster's parlor, the old man ignored the evidence that the two of us presented to him in the flesh. Instead, he talked to Father, as if Ben and I were not in the room at all. I was surprised by the respect that the older, more dignified man showed Father. "I have so thoroughly enjoyed those little essays of yours," he said to him.

It was only then that I began to realize that Father had a reputation as a naturalist and philosopher, who published his findings in learned journals and whose writings were widely respected. But the talk soon turned to Ben and me.

"Do they have their Latin?" the headmaster asked.

"A good beginning, I think, and Greek, too."

"We don't bother with Greek anymore," sighed the headmaster. "It is fine to teach it, you see, but old-fashioned to demand it of everyone. I am afraid it will be Latin to go next. What about their algebra?"

"In any sort of mathematics, algebra and geometry, they both excel."

The headmaster sat in silence, his fingertips pressed together, his eyes closed as if he might have fallen asleep for a minute. Then suddenly he jumped to his feet and asked with great excitement, "Can they run?"

"Is that a requirement?" Father asked.

"Oh, not at all. But we do expect them to exercise body as well as mind."

"Can you run, boys?" Father asked, smiling because he only rarely knew us to walk when running was possible.

85

"Oh, yes," I said. "Ben is the fastest in school and I am second."

"Not bed wetters?" the headmaster asked after he had taken his seat again.

"I should say not," said Father, who glanced vaguely in our direction. Perhaps that was something he had never thought to discuss with Mother. "They are both 12, after all," he said.

"Even at that age, there are a few," said the old man. "And it can cause such trouble, you know, at a boarding school."

In that instant, I wished that the two of us had been bed wetters, if it meant that we could stay home. I would have done anything to avoid the judgment of this doddering old man and the taunts of those sneering, laughing boys. But what I wanted did not matter any longer. Father and the headmaster were on their feet, standing by a window that looked across to the school buildings. "There he is," the old man said. "The boy Montrose that I told you about."

There, walking across an open space, standing tall above the other boys, was a redheaded boy, who seemed to have the attention of all the others around him. "A fine scholar as well as an athlete," the headmaster said. "He has made incredible progress here in just a short time, as I think your boys will."

Father stared out the window for the longest time. Finally he looked at the headmaster and extended his hand to him, sealing our fate with a handshake.

We were not to begin until the following fall. We had the whole summer before our departure, and I felt that it was to be the last summer of our childhood. Even Father, who had made the arrangements, felt the cloud that stood over us. Nell seemed particularly sad.

Once she turned to me at breakfast and announced, "Oh, I do wish that you did not have to go." She left the table because, I thought, she would have cried had she stayed. And I realized that of all my family I would miss Nell most.

She fell ill that spring and by summer she was extremely sick. Never very robust, she seemed to be drained by the slightest malady. And what began as a cold infected her lungs, and she lay in her bed for days at a time scarcely moving. The color left her cheeks. Her eyes seemed sunken and took on a darker hue. Charlotte, Ben, and I planted her green beans for her and told her that we expected her to harvest them. But as the full heat of summer fell upon us, she got no better, despite Father's strongest efforts.

Despite her weakened state, she smiled and laughed with us. She was, I thought, happy enough just to be in the midst of our family and the center of all our attention. The summer became a kind of vigil, with each of us taking turns at being company for her. We read her stories. We brought her the ripest berries and the reddest tomatoes. We drew comic pictures to amuse her. And all the while Father applied a variety of remedies in an effort to stop the disease that slowly seemed to consume her.

Nell's breathing became faster and shallower. One evening, as the summer sky darkened, Father placed small candles on her bare arms and shoulders and then covered the flames with inverted tumblers. "It creates a kind of vacuum," Father explained. "It has been done for centuries, although it is of dubious value. But I see no harm in trying."

Later I looked in through the open doorway as he placed his head upon Nell's chest and listened attentively. He looked up and said, more to himself than to me, "It is most certainly pneumonia, in both lungs now. We can but hope."

Over the next day, Nell improved and Father was encouraging. We all relaxed a little. Jackson Stone came by to demonstrate to Nell all the tricks that he could perform with an ordinary pocketknife. He whittled a little doll for her, which Charlotte clothed in scraps of cloth. Nell placed it by her nightstand.

But Nell soon began slipping further away, and Mother summoned Mrs. Dublin, who now seemed even older than she had before. When the poor woman left, sobbing into a lace handkerchief, I began to realize just how grave the situation had become. Nell slept all the time now. Even when I came in to see her, her eyes could only flutter open briefly before she fell back into a sleep.

One evening at the very end of summer, Mother summoned us all to stand beside Nell. "We cannot lose hope," she said, "but Nell may soon . . ."

She was stopped short by a bleating noise that came from Nell. "Bennnnnn," she uttered. "Ben, oh, Ben."

Ben went to her and bent over so that his ear almost touched her lips. She seemed to be babbling in a foreign tongue, her voice scarcely more than a whisper. I wondered why she had not called for me.

Ben bolted upright and ran from the room, out of the house and into the night. I chased after him, only to stumble when I caught a foot in a gopher hole in the middle of the meadow.

A crescent of moon cast an eerie light over the landscape, and as I grasped my twisted ankle, I could see Ben enter the woods. I got to my feet and tried to follow but I could no longer run. Ben emerged from the woods and rushed by, leaving me to hobble after him. When I finally reached Nell's bedside, she had been covered with mud. Smeared and splattered with the same moist earth, Ben stood over her and for the first time I saw him cry. "I am too late," he said. "Too late." ·

Mother pulled Ben back and hugged him to her. Nell's breath rattled in her chest. She opened her eyes and turned her head toward the window. There, framed in the upper pane, was a single bright star. It was Vega, I thought, Ben's guide star. Holding the wooden doll in both her hands, she fell asleep.

She did not die.

14

Away from Home

The pumpkins in our garden were large and ripe when it was time for Ben and me to leave for our new school. I had hoped that the day would never come. I was 12, but I had never been separated from Mother before, not even for a day. And it did not help that I thought a great deal about those fearsome boys at Hill in the Forest, most of them larger and older than I.

Ben did not seem to mind. In his mysterious past, he had been uprooted before. It must have seemed as natural to him as it would be to a tribe of nomads.

Mother did not cry when we left, but Nell and Charlotte did, with copious tears that almost made me cry as well, although I tried not to let anyone see that my eyes were brimming full. Father shook our hands heartily, as if we were like the young men in children's stories, setting out in the wide world to make our fortunes.

Nell took me aside and held both my hands. "I shall miss you," she said. She still was pale and weak, but she gripped my hands so hard that I dared not try to pull away.

The train was so crowded that we had to sit on our luggage in the entryway at one end of a car. We could see the New England foliage in all its colored glory from a window. "I wish we did not have to leave home," I said to Ben when we had settled into the rhythm of the rocking car.

"It is such a little journey," he said. "There are longer and more lonesome ones."

At the station, we were met by a short, balding man, who called us "lads," and spoke of us as "the Misters Westwood."

"You can call me Chippers," he said. "The real moniker is Chippendale, but Chippers is what all the lads call me, and you might as well follow suit. You are the last of the lads to arrive, you know. You'll just be settling in when your work begins in earnest. Then it will be all striving. Oh, yes, never you fear. There will be fun as well, but always striving and striving."

We followed him like obedient dogs to our quarters, where Chippers introduced us to our new roommates. "Let me introduce the two Misters Westwood to the two Misters Trevalian," he said. The room was a bare, dingily painted box on the second floor of one of the ivy-covered buildings. The Trevalians were two blond boys so nearly identical that you might have been looking at a single one of them with your eyes crossed. The two of them lay on their bunks, the one above

91

the other. They did not get up to greet us.

"Why do they always give us the new ones?" asked the Trevalian in the lower bunk.

"It may be because none of the older boys will have you," said a tall redheaded boy, who had just entered the room. He was the same one we had seen when we visited the school in the spring. "I am Montrose," he said, and he shook our hands. "Watch out for these two," he said, waving a hand toward the twins.

"Thinks he owns the place," said the Trevalian in the upper bunk, after Montrose left us. "But never mind. We'll soon break these two in."

The twins ordered us to sit down on the bunk opposite theirs. They began pacing back and forth before us.

"You," said one of the twins pointing at me, "will sweep the floor daily."

"And you," said the other addressing Ben, "will take out the laundry."

"And make up the beds every morning."

"And empty the trash as necessary."

"And sharpen the pencils and fill the inkwells."

"In return, we'll help you new boys settle in. We'll protect you from bullies."

"Where is your spending money?" asked one of them. Ben brought out a money clip with a few folded bills in it. "We'll take care of it for you," he said, and began counting. "Your father must be a pauper."

"Or a skinflint," added the other.

"And where is your money?" one of them asked me.

Ben might have turned over his allowance, but I was angry. I was not about to part with it easily. "You won't give it back!" I said.

"*He* might not give it back," said one of the twins

pointing to the other. "But you can trust *me* to take good care of it. You can have it back whenever you need it."

I looked to Ben for help, but he was unpacking his clothes and neatly putting them into a chest of drawers that he and I were to share. Reluctantly, I, too, handed over my folded clump of bills.

"Oh, you will get it back. You needn't cry," said one of them when he noticed that tears were welling up in my eyes.

When we went down to the dining hall for our evening meal, I noticed that Montrose sat at the head table. He was again the center of attention of several boys. I wondered if I would ever be as comfortable, as at home, as he appeared to be. The dining room had wood-lined walls and a fireplace large enough to walk into, if it were not filled with a blazing pile of logs. Flames shot up the chimney. Ben marveled at every detail: the carved wooden moldings, the clawshaped table legs, and a large painting of cows and cowherds alongside a rushing river.

It was all so foreign, so alien. For the first time in my life I found that I was crying in spite of myself when we all went to sleep that night. I stopped only when one of the Trevalians threw a shoe at me and shouted, "Stop that sniffling!" I could hear Ben's slow, steady breathing above me as I finally drifted off to sleep.

Classes began the next morning, soon after breakfast. I felt even more forlorn when I discovered that the instructors were cruel and unforgiving. But, to my surprise, Ben and I were both ahead of most of the boys in our classes.

When Mr. Bailey, the mathematics instructor, praised

Ben for correctly solving a particularly difficult problem, one of the Trevalians, sitting directly behind Ben, gave him a solid kick. The teacher noticed what had happened and grabbed the blond boy by the ear. As he led him out of the room to an unknown fate, he said, "Now just which of the Misters Trevalian are you? Is it Tweedledum or is it Tweedledee?"

"I didn't hurt him!" the boy shouted.

"And I am quite sure that a good paddling will not hurt you!" Mr. Bailey said.

After dinner that evening, Ben and I returned to our room, but the twins seemed to have disappeared. The two of us settled down at our writing tables to complete our homework, which included several pages of mathematical problems. When the twins finally arrived, they brought with them the heavy smell of tobacco smoke, although smoking was strictly against the rules.

One of the twins announced, "We expect that the two of you will be glad to share your homework with us."

Ben ignored them, but I rose to my feet in indignation. The twins were fully a foot taller than I was, but I paid that no attention. "You want us to help you cheat, and we won't do it!" I said.

"It's the least you can do in return for all the help we have given you," said one of the twins.

"I will not and you can't make me," I said. I found myself swinging wildly at the two of them, but not hitting either. One twin grabbed me from behind, and the second began pounding me with his fists. In my rage, I did not feel any pain, but I could feel that my nose had begun to bleed again. They would not stop.

But Ben had had enough. "Leave my brother alone,"

he said very quietly. The twins halted, surprised that not one, but two of us would show defiance. They pushed me to the ground and threw themselves at Ben, who was almost as tall as they were.

Ben grabbed the nearest boy by the shirt and pulled him close. With no effort at all, he lifted the boy over his head and tossed him across the room so that he landed in an upper bunk.

Looking suddenly rather frail, Ben sat down and continued his homework.

"Are you all right, Ben?" I asked.

"Just a little tired," he said. He was ashen. "Feel this," he said, and he placed my hand on his chest. I could feel his heart thumping wildly inside.

The Trevalian twins did their own homework that night.

15

Competition and Its Aftermath

The Trevalians did not bully us again. And slowly, in the smallest of steps, they even became friendly. They returned our money clips and insisted that we call them Johnny and Jim. And after a time, we even learned to tell them apart, although the differences between them were very slight. I suppose we had tamed them.

The word spread through the entire school of what Ben had done. He became a sort of hero. And it happened very quickly that we who arrived with no friends soon found ourselves with many. But I still suffered from homesickness at times, and I was very pleased when the two of us took the train back home for Thanksgiving.

Mother prepared a wonderful feast and Mrs. Dublin

and Jackson Stone joined us. I noticed that Nell appeared quite healthy again, and I was sad that I had to go back to school.

"Father," I said, the evening before we were to return. "Can't I stay here at home and go to Mrs. Winfield's with all of my friends?"

"And send Benjamin off all alone?" he asked.

"Ben could stay here, too," I insisted.

"Poor Roger," he said, placing a hand on the back of my head and ruffling my hair with affection. "This mind needs room enough to grow, and you won't find it here in a village schoolhouse."

He abruptly changed the subject. "What do you know of a boy named Montrose?" he asked.

"He is the most popular boy in school," I said. "We don't know him very well, Father. He is two years ahead of us."

"Two years," Father said, almost as if he were talking to himself. "Your headmaster has done quite a remarkable job with the boy. The family that found him sent him off to Hill in the Forest almost immediately."

"Found him?" I asked. "The way we found Ben?"

"It was much the same," he said. But he refused to say any more, despite my questions.

I went back to school, and in due course it came more and more to seem home to me. The older boys grew to seem less menacing, the adults less stern. The weather was unusually severe that winter, its blizzards leaving behind great drifts of snow that we boys time and again had to shovel away from doorways. There were days when we were indoors so much that we grew restless and would sneak outside at the height of a storm to pitch snowballs at one another.

On a dark afternoon of heavy, swirling snow, one

of the smallest of my classmates disappeared into the grayness of the woods. He was missing for more than an hour when the headmaster organized a search party of teachers and older boys to find him. Ben was chosen to go, but to my great disappointment, I was not allowed to join them.

Night had fallen, and how they managed to find the boy in the dark, I do not know. But Ben and Montrose brought the little fellow to the common room of our residence hall, where logs sparked and snapped in a huge fireplace. Mr. Bailey soon followed them and ordered dry clothes for the boy who lay shivering in a wet puddle of snow that had melted on the carpet. "He is cold as ice," Mr. Bailey said, "but alive thanks to those two young men."

"He was completely buried," Ben told me later. "We could not see him at all, but we knew where to find him. He was a warm place in the snow."

That evening at dinner Montrose and Ben were given seats of honor at the front table. And after our meal, all of us got to our feet and raised up such a cheer that I was sure it could be heard by the rescued boy who was sleeping in his room three floors above us.

Gradually the days lengthened, the snow melted away, and overnight the tiny red and green buds along the branches of trees burst open into spring.

Mother and Father, Charlotte and Nell came to visit during the weekend of the annual track meet. Both Ben and I were entered in the races. There was no one in our class quicker than Ben, but he had no endurance. I was the opposite and was able to run for miles without feeling tired at the finish.

My race began in the chill of the morning. I stood

with 20 or more of the younger boys all bumping together to be closest to the starting line. "Ready," the starter shouted. "Get set. Go!" Amid much jostling, I raced to the front. We were to run around a dirt track and then turn off into a field, through a bit of hilly forest along a creek and then back again for a final lap to the finish line. But I had no idea about strategy and did not think to save my strength. "Slow down! Slow down!" I could hear Ben shouting.

Hearing footsteps behind me, I moved even faster. But when I reached the first of the hills, I was already winded and several boys passed me. My legs became painfully heavy and I began falling hopelessly behind.

One of the wonders of cross-country racing is that for every uphill run, a downhill run still awaits you. I caught up with my breath, my legs lightened, and the path actually seemed to give spring to my feet. I began catching the boys who had passed me, and when I crested the last of the hills, I could see that there were only two ahead of me, one a dark-haired boy about my own size and the other a tall, blond fellow who moved with long and easy strides.

I was determined to catch them. The dark-haired boy kept looking back at me, and every time he did, I narrowed the distance between us even more until finally I overtook him. As we reached the dirt track for the final lap, only the blond boy was ahead of me. With only a few hundred yards left, I was so close to him that I could have touched him. He turned his head around and appeared surprised, even wounded to see me so close so near the end of the race. He stumbled. And I passed him, with only a short dash left to the finish. But then I felt a terrible cramp in my right leg and I fell to the ground. With difficulty, I got to my feet and began limping forward, but before I could reach the ribbon stretched across the finish line, first the blond boy and then the dark-haired one passed me. I fell across the line and a dozen boys had to skip over me or dodge around me before someone reached out a hand to help me to my feet. It was Montrose, his red hair blowing in the breeze. "I did not know you had that in you," he said.

Montrose was the champion runner of the school, racing against the older boys in the 100-yard dash. Ben ran against younger boys in the same event. By afternoon, Ben proved his skill by winning two separate heats that led to the younger boys' final, one of the last events of the day.

I stood with Mother, Father, Charlotte, and Nell as Ben and five other boys crouched down for the final race. Already Ben seemed pale and winded, but he lined up gamely along with our classmates, several of whom had learned to crouch low the way the truly great sprinters of our day did.

"Ready. Set. Go!"

Within a few strides, Ben was in the lead, and he widened the gap with every step he took. Unlike distance runners, who race with a long, loping gait like a horse on the gallop, Ben moved his legs like pistons, his feet pulverizing the earth as he leaned toward the finish.

Amid tumultuous shouting, he fell to the dirt and lay still for a moment before rising to his feet with great difficulty.

Chippers, carrying a large stopwatch in his hand, rushed up to Ben's sprawling figure. "A half second," he said, again and again. "A full half second off the record, lad."

Ben wearily allowed himself to be helped to his feet. By then Father had rushed up to him. "Are you all right, son?" he asked.

"Fine," Ben said, without much conviction. "I will be fine."

I was surprised to see that Ben was taller than Mother and Charlotte, who hugged him to her. I was embarrassed for Ben, but he did not appear to mind it.

By the time of the final event of the day, Ben appeared rested. He watched with interest as Montrose easily beat the other older boys in the 100-yard dash, just as Ben had finished far ahead of the others in his race.

The headmaster came down from the reviewing stand, I thought to congratulate Montrose for his victory. But instead he pointed to the stand where we were sitting as he talked excitedly, his hands flapping wildly all the while. The headmaster conferred briefly with Chippers, who, along with Montrose, walked over to where we were standing.

Chippers spoke to Ben. "My watch tells me, Mr. Westwood, that yours is the fastest time of the day for the 100 among all the classes. And the headmaster has suggested that you might like to try your luck against Mr. Montrose."

"The boy is far too tired," Father objected. "I cannot allow it."

"I am fine," Ben said. "I think I could run again."

Montrose grinned. "What a race this will be!" he said. He seemed winded, more so than one might expect several minutes after a sprint. But he took several deep breaths and then raised his long legs one after the other, running in place, as if to prove himself fit for another round of competition.

I thought that both boys looked pale. Father certainly must have seen this as well, but he was no match for the boys' determination to race against each other, and gave his reluctant consent.

All the boys in the school, their parents and guests, and all of the instructors crowded along the dirt track as Ben and Montrose walked to the starting line again. Both of them had sideburns and the faint signs of beards and mustaches. Except for their coloring, they were a matched pair, tall and lean, and already more men than boys. How could it be that Ben was growing up so much faster than I was? I wondered.

"Get ready!" Ben looked up from his crouch and leaned toward the finish line. "Get set!" Every muscle in his body pulled tight. "Go!"

The two boys matched each other step for step, their legs churning like dynamos in a blur of electric motion. Halfway down the course, Montrose moved ahead by inches, then half a stride and then a full one. Both boys crumpled to the ground at the finish.

"A tenth of a second!" I heard Chippers shout. "A tenth of a second!"

Father had to push through the crowd to get to the boys. Ben flailed about, trying to catch his breath, but Montrose lay perfectly still. Father reached for the red-haired boy's throat to feel for the pulse, and then he put his head to the boy's chest. "Back up and be still!" Father commanded the crowd. We moved away. Father put his head to Montrose's chest again.

"I hear nothing," he said. "Nothing."

Montrose was dead.

16

Recovery

Ben was very ill. It was several days before Father agreed that it was safe to put him on a train home, so delicate was Ben's condition. I stayed on to finish the term, but the whole school was in mourning. It was a somber time, even though Father assured me that Ben would recover.

When I finally returned home, Father greeted me at the station in his automobile, a new one equipped with running boards. When we arrived at the house, I rushed into a little ground floor parlor that Mother had converted to a bedroom for Ben. He sat in bed, propped up by pillows and with his mattress blanketed in notebooks and texts. He had lost weight and his already lean features seemed more gaunt than ever, even hollow.

When he saw me, he commanded me to look at a notebook he was working on, one filled with mathematical formulas and elaborate sketches.

"What is that?" I asked, pointing to a set of lines that he had crosshatched and shaded to look like a slender cylinder.

"It is a rocket ship," Ben said. "A craft for escaping earth's gravity."

"It's impossible," I said.

"One day it will be possible," he said. "Until then our dreams will have to carry us away."

For the first part of summer, Father did not allow Ben to leave the house at all. It was Charlotte who nursed him and fed him and became his legs for him. Sometimes he would send her off to the pond to fetch plants that he wanted for a collection. She sharpened his pencils and tidied his papers. She saw to it that his diet was rich in fresh fruits and vegetables that she raised for him in our garden.

Nell and I, when our chores were done, would often wander up to the pond, but it seemed an empty journey without Charlotte and Ben to join us. By the end of the season, Ben began taking short walks and then longer ones. Once Jackson Stone carried Ben up to the pond on his broad back. They were a ridiculous sight, with Ben's long legs sticking out in front of them as Jackson staggered up the trail.

Ben insisted that he could walk back down to the house by himself, but he seemed gravely tired. His health was so very brittle that I finally spoke to Father about it.

"Will Ben ever become completely well?" I asked.

"He will recover, slowly. Have patience."

"But will he ever be entirely well?" I persisted.

He shook his head. "Ben and Nell are not like the rest of us. Theirs is a fragile strength, easily broken. They are like animals that can run at great speed over a short distance but die if a predator should press them beyond endurance. It is, I believe, a weakness from birth."

"But he will be fine again, won't he?" I asked.

Father rubbed his chin and observed me for a moment before deciding to go ahead. "He will live and live well. But I am afraid he will not live long. You saw what happened to Montrose, and how close we came to losing Nell. One day, sooner than we would like, they all will be taken from us."

"But will it be very soon?" I asked.

"No," he said. "Not very soon. Not if we are careful to tend well to them."

I went back to Hill in the Forest School by myself that fall. When I came home for Christmas, it was Ben who drove the car to the station to pick me up. He was even taller now, with square features and a beard that needed shaving. I, too, had been growing, but not as fast as he. "We have some surprises for you, Roger," he said as he gripped my hand.

At dinner, he announced them. "I am going to enter Harvard College next month," he said. "It is all arranged, I have been accepted." He smiled.

It was Charlotte's turn. "And Ben and I are going to marry in the spring," she said. I should have been startled by both revelations but I was not. It seemed right that my brilliant brother start college before me. Ben, who had once seemed the same age and size as I, had grown somehow many years older. And when

I looked at him and at Charlotte, I saw before me a grown man and woman, no longer in the least children.

As they had planned, in the sun-warmed air of late spring, we gathered together under a canopy that father had raised in our meadow, and the two were wed.

After the ceremony, the two of them left by train to a small house near the university, not far from where the poet Henry Wadsworth Longfellow once lived. At the station, we were all in the highest of spirits, but as soon as the train pulled away Father became unusually solemn. And when I asked him what was the matter, he did not reply and only shook his head slowly and sadly.

Back home, Nell and I walked together along familiar paths. She noticed everything, the blossoms on the trees, the chipmunks and the squirrels, the tiny flowers underneath our feet as we sauntered through the meadow.

I suppose I thought that I would one day marry Nell, but I was but a boy of 14 and would have been afraid to say it. I could not imagine anything that would make me as happy as being with her as I was that day.

She turned to me as if she knew what I was thinking. "It can never be," she said. "We cannot ever be like Ben and Charlotte."

"Why not?" I blurted out.

"Look at me," she said. And when I looked into her dark eyes I could see the same woeful little girl she had been when we found her in the county home.

"No!" she said. "You must really look at me."

Inexplicably, I began to notice things about Nell that I had never stopped to see before. Like Ben, she too had become older than I was — taller and more grown up. Here and there, I could see white hairs mixed in with the black. The skin had begun to crinkle about her eyes.

"I grow old," she said. "There will not be much time."

She took my hand in hers as we continued our walk. Now I was the glum one, but she seemed relieved, even happy.

"I will love you forever and ever," she said. "And when you are old, you will remember me."

17

A Revelation

Truly if there is a time when childhood ends, that summer was such a time for me. Nell was often busy helping Mother with chores. And when she was free, she was strangely distant. Without Ben, I was alone much of the day and found myself moping for hours at a time. Nothing that I could think of doing seemed to satisfy me. To my own surprise, I longed for the day when I would leave for school again.

A few days before I was to depart, Father guided me into his library. "Nell asked me to talk to you," he said as we took our seats in two plump chairs.

I felt the color rising in my face; my forehead prickled. I wanted to say something, to explain what I was feeling but the words slithered from me, like the frogs we found at the pond.

"You have seen the changes in Nell and in Ben," he said softly. "Perhaps now you can grasp how different they are from the rest of us."

"You speak as if Nell and Ben were of a different species," I protested.

Father did not reply for what seemed like several minutes. He looked downward as if he were studying the tips of his shoes, which I noticed were scuffed and stained.

"In a way, what you say is true," he said. He appeared to be weighing just how much he could tell me. He raised his head high and for a long time gazed directly into my eyes as if searching for a sign that I might be worthy of a further explanation. Suddenly, he smiled and became almost cheerful.

"Nell is right. It is time that you learn what she and Ben have known for quite some time. I should have told you long ago. If I had known that you cared for Nell, I would have done so. It has been a mistake to wait so long."

He eased back in his chair and pulled a pipe from the jacket he wore, but did not light it. "You know that I am a New Englander, much more of one than you. A Yankee through and through. I don't go in for sentimental babble. I am from a long, long line of those who believe that a person ought to keep his feelings to himself. I always thought my parents, my family, to be a cold people. So cold that I fled from them, and against their advice studied medicine under a country doctor and became one myself.

"But even here I see our neighbors sharing little of themselves. We Yankees take our troubles with us to the grave. But then we take our joys with us, too. Perhaps it is time to become a little less New England."

He jabbed the air with his pipe as if to punctuate his speech. "Let me start with the most surprising fact of all. I know of seven wild children, who were found in this region in the spring of 1913."

"Seven?" I asked.

"Eight, if I include that pitiful creature you children found floating in the cave the following summer. And one more if I add the one that you saw floating in the pond just after Ben arrived."

I was totally surprised, just as he said I would be. "I knew of Ben and Nell and the Crispin boy and the one other, whose parents spoke to you at the wedding. But who were the others?"

"There was the Keefe child, found 30 miles from here to the west on the other side of the mountain. The Connors' girl. They all suffered from one or another terrible defect and simply failed to thrive. The Blyleven child, the one whose parents you spoke of, lingered on for months. He died in the fall of 1913 after a long illness."

"What did they die of?" I asked.

"They were ill-made, all of them. They were all flawed anatomically, you could say." Father walked over to a shelf and pulled a volume from it. As he began leafing through its pages, I recognized it as one of his own notebooks.

"I learned of the Montrose boy only much later," he said as he ran his fingers over a page near the back of the volume. "He was the last that I discovered, but long after he was found hiding under a cabin several miles to the west of us. How many more there might have been, we will never be sure."

He placed the open book on his writing table and carefully pulled a set of spectacles from his breast pocket.

They were small glasses, with rims of gold, and he gingerly unfolded them, perched them on his nose and secured the side pieces over his ears.

"Here it is," he said after leafing through several pages. He pointed to the entry. " 'October 19, 1913,' " he read. " 'Called out of bed in the early morning hours,' " he halted.

"Here, you may read it for yourself," he said.

The book smelled of chemicals, both sweet and foul, the strongest odor that of burnt sulfur. Each page was in Father's fastidious, almost miniature, hand. "Out loud, Roger, if you don't mind," Father said.

I did as he asked:

" 'Called out of bed in the early morning hours. I had had little enough sleep. The man at the door said he was Matthew Blyleven and that he had come a full day's journey to fetch me. His son was dying, he said.

" 'Having little choice in the matter, I dressed myself as quickly as I could and left with him. I tied the man's horse to my buggy and insisted that Blyleven ride with me so that he might sleep if he was able. But he did not sleep at first. He was much too excited and agitated. Instead he told me a story that is similar to one that I heard more than once before. Like most, his tale began in the spring with a powerful beacon of light, a heavy scented smoke, and then the appearance of a naked child, unscratched and without a burn, wild as an animal but surprisingly easy to be tamed. Unlike some of the others, the Blyleven boy fared very poorly from the start. And now his condition had worsened and he lay near death, almost unable to draw a breath.

" 'If the boy were still alive as we rode through the night, perhaps I might be able to help. After relating these events to me, the poor man, who probably had never said so much in his life to a complete stranger, slumped off to sleep. "Little Matty," he kept crying softly from his slumber. "Little Matty."

" 'I too began to feel a drowsiness come over me and I longed for sleep, but slapped myself and splashed water on my face to keep awake. I dared not halt. When the dawn came, I roused Blyleven and took my turn at sleeping.

" 'Finally we arrived at the Blyleven farm. Within a minute of walking into that humble man's house, I knew the boy's problem. I could hear it from across the room. His arteries vibrated with every heartbeat, giving off a rumbling sound, or bruit, that I immediately recognized as the direst of symptoms. It was a sign of an obstruction to the flow of the blood leaving the heart.

" 'I administered one of my concoctions, an extract made from foxglove, and it appeared at first to help. His breathing settled down, I thought. But there were limits to how much I might give a boy of his size. And the relief that my remedy gave him was not great enough. By the next day, he worsened and died that night.

" 'I asked the boy's family for permission to conduct an autopsy. I pressed them to allow me to arrange a full postmortem examination at a Boston hospital, but in their grief the family refused to let the body be transported. When I persisted in my request, they granted me permission to do a limited examination of my own, if I could complete it that very night. In a storage shed, under a kerosene lamp, without anyone else to assist me, I conducted the study using the few instruments I brought with me and employing every bit of my medical knowledge and training.

" 'I was surprised at the extent to which the boy's anatomy was defective. I was baffled that he had lived as long as he had. The major vessels were not properly joined to his heart, which had responded by growing too large for the body. The liver, spleen, and stomach were also imperfectly connected to their blood supplies. In a phrase, the boy's body was poorly crafted. I wished that I could have examined the brain, but it was impossible under the circumstances. There was nothing left but to sew up the Y-shaped incision I had made in the abdomen and return the intact body to the family. Under a canopy of stars, we buried the small form in a grave that Matthew Blyleven had dug for his son in the middle of a circle of burnt earth, where the family had discovered him.' "

I stopped reading where the entry ended and looked up from the book.

"All of them were found within a region of several hundred square miles," Father said. "Even Montrose, although the family that found him quickly transported him to their home in Boston and later sent him off to school. I realized that they were not lost children at all. And now I believe they were sent here with the purpose of our finding and raising them."

"Sent by whom?" I asked. "Sent from where? Surely they did not come falling out of the sky."

"I do not know," he said. "I doubt that *I* will ever know with certainty. But there is more I need to tell you. That creature you found floating in the muddy water of a cave almost a year later was almost perfectly preserved. It was a human form although an ill-made one. It was as soft and uncalloused as a newborn, but many times the size.

"Like the Blyleven boy, its internal organs were not

in the necessary proportions. Surely that is also true of the others."

"Ben and Nell, too?" I blurted out. "But they are alive. Perhaps they are different."

Father shook his head. "You have seen the signs of it yourself. How easily they tire. How infirm they are. And for other reasons, perhaps, they already show signs of advancing age. I have read of such cases of accelerated aging in the medical literature. But such reports are extremely rare. I fear that Ben and Nell will have shortened lives, like Montrose. They will be like meteors, bright and full of light, but quick expiring."

"Surely, we can do something," I said.

"Oh, we can care for them. Nurse them. Watch them closely and perhaps delay the outcome that I fear. But it will not change the underlying imperfection in their physical nature."

Father's face seemed gray and old now. I reached across to him and placed a hand on his shoulder.

"Everything will be fine," I tried to assure him, in the same manner that he always had reassured me in my minor childhood calamities. I was filled with the optimism common to healthy young men and women, whose futures seem to stretch out before them endlessly and with infinite possibility.

He handed me his notebook. "I give you this to keep," he said. And as he did so he smiled, as if he had handed me a heavy burden that he had been carrying.

"I am giving over to you a mystery," he said. "It comforts me to think that you might be the one who will finally solve it."

18

Clippings

I was happy to be back again at school, although at first I found myself missing Ben. But soon I was too busy at sports and my schoolwork to feel any pangs of sorrow. At Thanksgiving we all gathered at Charlotte and Ben's little house in Cambridge for a feast. Nell seemed more beautiful and yet more frail than she had been, and I felt terribly shy to be with her again.

"I intend to be a doctor one day," I announced to her. "I will find a cure for this illness that afflicts you and Ben."

"There is no illness to be cured," she said. "It is just that I tire more easily than others."

I had been learning to play the game of chess at school and offered to teach it to her. "Such a complicated game," she said, as I finally completed my description of the moves permitted each of the pieces.

Although a beginner, I caught on to the game very quickly and was soon the champion of my class. And I was a little surprised in my first game with Nell to hear her ask after no more than a dozen moves, "What is it that you say when you can capture the other player's king?"

"Checkmate," I said.

"Then 'Checkmate!'" she said, with great ceremony.

I looked at the wooden pieces, most of which were crowded tightly together near the middle of the board, and I began to laugh very loudly. Nell began laughing, too. And soon it felt as if we were friends again, and the pain of her changing so quickly did not seem to hurt quite as deeply.

At dinner, Charlotte and Ben had an announcement. "We are going to have a baby," my sister said. I began to bang my knife and fork together the way all the boys did at Hill in the Forest School when momentous announcements were made, like the day we entered the Great War in Europe. Nell and Ben and even Mother joined in, but Father sat quietly and simply patted Charlotte on the hand.

"Where is Jackson Stone?" I asked later, when the pies and cakes were being served.

"Gone off to war, I am afraid," Father said.

"Jackson will show those Huns a thing or two," I said, mimicking the way all my schoolmates talked about the war against Germany.

"They are humans, too," Ben objected. "I could not bring myself to kill another, no matter what side he were on."

Charlotte began to bang her knife and fork together, and was soon joined by Mother and Nell. I was embarrassed and very glad to change the subject. I did not know what a warmonger I had become. And later in the evening, when Nell and I broke the wishbone together, I wished that the war would be over soon and that our friend Jackson would come safely home.

Ben showed me his study, a tiny cubicle of a room, filled with books on hundreds of subjects. Every inch of space was cluttered with papers and volumes and journals, and yet Ben seemed to be able to find whatever he needed amid the rubble.

"Here," he said, handing me a kind of scrapbook. "I thought you might enjoy looking at this."

The book was filled with letters and yellowed newspaper clippings from around the country. A short item from Bend, Oregon, caught my attention. The sheriff there was investigating complaints about the remains of what was called a "pig-boy," whose preserved little corpse was on display at a carnival sideshow. "Pig-Boy a Fraud," proclaimed a headline, followed in smaller type by "Corpse Is Not Human, County Coroner Says." The date on the article was October 30, 1915.

Another clipping, dated a year later, talked about the death of a wild boy who had been found three years before just outside of Denver, Colorado. The boy had never been allowed to leave a home for the mentally disturbed. The story quoted the director of the asylum, who said that at the time of the boy's discovery it was widely believed he had been raised by wolves. The director said there was no proof of that, and he was convinced that the child was simply deranged and had run away from those who were caring for him.

Still another item described the sighting of a meteor shower over the Olympic peninsula in Washington State in the spring of 1913.

The letters were from places like California and Wisconsin and the Carolinas. And each in a different way described the discovery of a child or children, lost and naked, adopted into families or shipped off to homes for the insane or dead from exposure or disease.

"There were hundreds of us," Ben said with a smile.

"Hundreds?" I said doubtfully. "Hundreds?"

"Perhaps even more," he said. "There might have been thousands. After all, I have limited my inquiries to the United States. Not very many of us have survived, I am afraid."

"How can you be so certain that these are all connected?" I asked.

"There are clues in all these cases," he said. "The dates, the circumstances. You know the details. A burnt circle of earth. A metallic material that crumbles to dust when it is touched. In some cases, I am only guessing, but even there the evidence is mounting that my speculation is correct. I have found over 300 such reports, and of those there may be more than 100 survivors, but my research is continuing."

"But w-w-why?" I found myself stuttering. "Who has sent them and for what purpose?"

"Who has sent *us*?" Ben repeated, reminding me that he was indeed one of *them*. "Next you will be asking what kinds of creatures we might be. I do not yet know the answer. If I am given enough time, perhaps I will be able to find out."

19

A New Generation

My brother Ben was such a remarkable student that in two years of college he completed the work that most labor at for four. Even before he was graduated, he published papers on astronomy that soon earned him a worldwide reputation. The pages of each were filled with mathematical formulas as foreign to me as the hieroglyphics of Egypt. He became a member of the Harvard faculty at about the time my sister Charlotte gave birth to a baby girl, Katarina.

My own achievements in school seemed rather dim when compared to the luster of Ben's. And yet I, too, was a gifted student, although in a much more modest way than my adopted brother. With Father's help, in the fall of 1918, I was admitted to Harvard College at the age of 15, the youngest by a year in my class.

I lived in Cambridge and could spend my weekends with Ben and Charlotte and my little niece. From the moment of her birth, Katarina was flush and strong and alert. She had Charlotte's physical hardiness and Ben's gleaming intelligence.

Mother and Nell often came to help Charlotte with the new baby, and it was Nell who reported that Katarina's first word was not "Mama" or "Papa" or "Cat," but "Rahl." She was just a few months old when she first pronounced it, while Nell held her by a sunlit window. I was puzzled at first, convinced that it was no word at all but only gibberish.

"It means 'star,' " Nell explained to me rather matter-of-factly.

"In what language?" I laughed. "And why would she say 'star' in the fullness of daylight?"

"The sun is a star as you very well know," Nell said. "And I am not sure how it is that I know that 'Rahl' means star, but I am sure that it does, proving what a bright little niece we have."

When I mentioned this to Ben, he, too, seemed surprised. " 'Lo-say-rahl,' " he said. "It is the name for the sun in the language of a dream I had when I was younger. It means 'the warming star.' I had a similar name for the star Vega, which was 'no-say-rahl,' the 'guide star.' But Katarina's saying it must be a coincidence. We can make whatever sense we like from the babbling of a baby."

Even before she could speak in sentences, Katarina sat by herself for hours, leafing through books as if she were actually reading them, which, of course, was impossible. Even before she was one year old, Ben gave her a child's book of astronomy, full of pictures of planets and charts of the stars and solar system.

"This is home," I explained to her as I pointed at the third planet from the sun.

"Star rahl, rahl star," Katarina said, pointing to the sun itself — the only star in the solar system.

When Katarina was two, her twin brothers Robert and Charles were born — Bobby and Chaz as we soon called them. The little dark-haired boys were as precocious as their sister, and within a year or so, the three of them were chattering endlessly, sometimes in a language of their own devising.

One afternoon, as I sat in the kitchen of Charlotte and Ben's house, with my course work spread out upon the table, Katarina rushed up to me with her hands behind her back. "Watch my trick, Uncle Roger," she insisted.

I had noticed that day that she seemed to love nothing more than rolling out long snakes of clay and then coiling them into hollow cylinders. She spent many minutes trying to teach her brothers to do this as well, but they had little patience.

Now she held in front of her a closed-off cylinder she had fashioned from her clay. "Look at the baby, Uncle Roger," she chortled. "Look at the baby."

I turned the object in my hands and studied it appreciatively. For such a small child, she had taken great pains to make the coils even.

"This is not a baby," I started to say.

"Yes, it is," she said, snatching it from my hands and throwing the clay to the ground. The object split open on impact, revealing a tiny ceramic doll that Mother had given her.

"Oh," I said. "Then it is a baby. But why have you wrapped it up so tight in your clay?"

"So that it could sleep well on its journey, Uncle Roger," Katarina said.

"Well, I am very sorry that your creation is broken, Katey," I said, wondering whether or not she had heard the story about Ben and Nell and the other wild children.

"It was not broken," she explained. "The baby was ready to wake up."

When I described Katarina's game with clay to Charlotte, my sister insisted that she and Ben had never told their children about the strange creature we found floating in the pond many years before. "They know so much without being told," she said. "I sometimes wonder where this knowledge comes from and whether it was intended for some useful purpose. When I ask Ben about it, he smiles at me and says they are 'destiny's children.' But it is worrisome to me, how much they know."

My own college days were coming to a close. Still determined to become a doctor, I was a student of biology and chemistry, fascinated by cells of plants and animals and the parts within those cells. Sometimes I saw myself as a watchmaker, devoted to repairing an almost hopelessly complicated timepiece. If you took the living mechanism apart, the little pieces would scatter and could not be put back together again. But even then I knew that the physical weakness that troubled Ben and Nell was a defect in the manufacture of the smallest of parts, and I was determined to master the workings of cells, if that was needed to cure their condition.

Nell, whose hair was now mostly gray, seemed healthy enough, but Ben had begun to weaken. There were periods when he was confined to bed for days at a time;

and to leave the house at all, he often required a wheelchair. Father was worried about him and tried to devise a regimen of diet and the most gentle of exercise in an effort to strengthen him. On every visit, Father would listen to Ben's chest with a stethoscope and would conclude with great hopefulness, "No change, no change. That is quite an encouraging sign, that there is no change." But I knew that he meant that there was no improvement, either.

On the other hand, the children were exceptionally hardy. About them, Father could honestly rhapsodize. "They are as healthy as little colts and little fillies," he would say with great delight.

On one steamy summer afternoon, just after I graduated from college and was about to begin a year of laboratory study, I sat with Ben and Charlotte in the little yard behind their house. Not far from us, Katarina, who was scarcely four, had climbed high into an oak tree. She seemed to have an uncanny sense of balance and showed no sign of slipping or falling, even when she found herself clinging to branches that bent beneath her weight.

"She's a monkey," I said, my face I am sure revealing my concern for Katarina's safety.

"Well, a primate, in any case," Ben said, not in the least troubled about Katarina's location.

I watched with even more terror as Chaz and Bobby began scrambling up the tree in imitation of their sister. They were just a few months past two and I marveled at their climbing ability. But as they climbed higher, I could stand it no longer. I jumped to my feet and shouted, "Chaz, watch out or you'll fall!"

Perhaps, if I had said nothing, he would have continued up the tree without incident. But Chaz looked down at me and his feet swung out from beneath him, leaving him clinging to a branch by only one tiny hand. For a moment he hung there, only to lose his grip and fall to the earth below with an awful thud. Even before I could reach his crumpled body, Katarina was kneeling over him, speaking to him in that secret language of theirs that had no kinship to English.

"He will be all right," Katarina assured me. "I can see it in his eyes."

I, too, examined Chaz's eyes, looking for signs of brain swelling that would be expected to affect the size of his pupils. I had learned this from Father. My nephew's eyes were fine, their dark centers closed down to tiny points as he gazed up at the bright, but hazy summer sky. Charlotte and I felt his limbs for broken bones.

"You were right in your diagnosis," I said to Katarina. "But how did you know about the eyes?"

"I just knew," she said simply, shaking her dark brown curls.

When the adults regained their composure, the children began starting up the tree again. I rose to my feet with the intention of stopping them.

But Ben grabbed my arm and said forcefully, "Let them go. They will know how high they can go with safety."

For the rest of the afternoon, I watched them warily, but said nothing. The three of them climbed breathtakingly high, but without incident. I was at ease again only when they descended to the earth.

20

Preparation for a Journey

Y ou don't look well," I said to my brother. It was
a late autumn afternoon. The light beamed into
Ben's study from the garden and reflected off the polished wood and metal fittings of his wheelchair. He
rarely moved without it now. I was a vigorous 19 years
old, and he could not have been much older. But his
skin was wrinkled and ashen, his hair completely gray.
Still, as he spoke, his eyes darted back and forth, a
sign of his lively intelligence.

"I have not *been* well for some time," he said. "Nor
do I think that I will ever be well again. You have
been after me for months to find someone to assist
here with our chores, and I have found just the right
person to do that and a good deal more. He has been
waiting to meet you."

Into the room at that precise moment, laughing at my look of surprise, came our childhood friend and one-time nemesis Jackson Stone.

I noticed that he walked with a slight limp, but he was still tall and strong and shook my hand quite vigorously as if he were pumping water from a well. He appeared to take pleasure in pulling up a trouser leg and rapping on a wooden limb that he walked on in place of his own. "It is my souvenir of the war," he said, still smiling. I must have had a tragic look on my face, because he added, "Almost as good as the real thing."

"I will need the help of both of you," Ben said. He spoke with considerable effort, his voice scarcely louder than a whisper, as if that were all the breath he could muster. "I want your help in bringing together a large group of *us*."

I knew that he meant the wild children, now all grown old as he was. "You speak of yourself as if you were something other than human," I said.

"I *am* an alien," Ben said. His jacket hung loose over his arms, so that when he waved them he looked like a prehistoric bird, flapping its loose-skinned wings at takeoff. "We are creatures from out there," he said. He lifted his arm weakly in the direction of the ceiling, toward the stars that he had spent much of his life studying.

"You cannot know that," I said.

"The evidence is not direct, but I know. It is an inescapable conclusion, as all my research has convinced me."

"But surely you are human or you could not have fathered a child," I persisted.

"Enough like humans for that," he said. "We are not monsters or beasties, surely, but humans of another kind. Perhaps, we are simply a tribe of people that took a separate path a long time ago. But not so long ago or so far astray from the rest of you that we are any less human than you are."

I sat silently, not knowing what else to say. Jackson got to his feet again and began pacing back and forth in the narrow space beside us, as if he were practicing the use of his artificial leg.

"Please promise that you will help me," Ben said to me. "There is very little time."

Just then, almost as if on cue, his three children burst in upon us. First came Katarina, not yet even five, followed by her two matching brothers. They all began climbing onto Benjamin's wheelchair, and I leaned forward thinking that I ought to keep them away from my ailing, adopted brother. But he welcomed them, spreading his winglike arms to enfold the three of them. As quickly as they had come, the children bounced to the floor, shaking the wooden planks with every step, jostling the pictures on the walls, and sending papers flying as they romped away.

"I will miss them," Ben said absently.

"Miss them?" I asked with considerable alarm. "Surely you don't think you are going to be leaving, that you are about to . . ." I could not pronounce the final word.

"Yes, I will die," he said, completing my thought for me. "Not very soon, but far sooner than you. Yet I was speaking, not of my dying, but of their going away, the three of them. On the long journey."

"What are you talking about?" I asked, feeling in

that moment a rage at the thought that these our children — and I did consider them mine — might be taken away.

"It was decided for us," he said, "long ago and far away. The evidence is there if only you choose to listen. It is what all my research has convinced me of. They," he said, turning his head in the direction just taken by the children, "are not of either kind. Not of yours and Charlotte's people. Not of Nell's and mine. They are a hybrid race, strengthened for having strayed here."

It was too ridiculous to believe. I rose to my feet and moved toward his chair, so that I towered over him, my fist tightly clenched. Jackson put a gentle hand on my shoulder. Never in all our days together had I ever been as angry with Ben, not even in those first weeks when his wild presence had so thoroughly and permanently disrupted our lives.

"Sit down and listen," Jackson commanded me.

I looked at my kindly and enfeebled brother and I was filled with remorse for my anger. As Jackson had bid me, I collapsed into my chair. Ben continued in a voice so raspy and faint that I had to lean far forward to hear him.

"As you know, I have been writing to people all over the country for a few years now. And many of my scientific friends have helped to make inquiries on my behalf. I could not undertake the traveling that was in some cases necessary to confirm the cases and identify the other wild children.

"But I quickly came to a dead end. I could not calculate where we had come from or why. And there seemed nothing to do with the information I collected but put it into a book and then put the volume on a shelf and forget the matter.

"And yet all of my life, from the beginning with our family, I knew that I had come from the stars. I would feel such a great sadness and longing just standing beneath a clear night sky. We all have felt homesickness. But this was a feeling even more intense: a loneliness, a longing for a home I never knew.

"Even as a small boy in Mother's house, I kept having dreams, always the same. I would feel a great coldness come over me, followed by a cloak of utter dark. At first I thought that I might be dreaming of my own death. My health has always been poor, and I thought it quite natural for my sleeping brain to conjure up these strange images.

"But I had no fear of death, and the dream kept recurring. And I began to notice strange details within it. There were in the dark bright points of light. And after a while, I began to notice a vast triangle, like a cluster of stars, a constellation. Yet search as I would through maps of the heavens, I saw no constellation quite like this one. I even gave names to the brightest of the stars. I called them 'the guide star,' 'the home star,' and 'the warming star.'

"Later, I noticed that in these dreams I seemed to be traveling within the constellation itself, the pattern of the three bright stars shifting as I moved among them. Always in these dreams, I felt my arms tightly bound to my chest, my knees pulled up against me, as if I were in the womb. But I was surrounded by a transparent shell that allowed me to see all around.

"I was alive in these dreams, but in a suspended state. The silence was total, not even broken by breathing or the pulse beat of my heart. The dreams ended in a burst of light so intense that it was blinding.

"I began to have still another repeating dream, which was really a variation of the first. I stood in a crowd of people, not in a city, but in a clearing in a heavy forest, almost a jungle. Above me, I could see a bright sun and feel its warmth upon me. Suddenly a soft substance would rise up from the earth to envelop me, pressing so tightly that the wind was squeezed from my chest and I could not catch another breath.

"The details were unusually sharp. I could make out every single face in the crowd. I saw the chips and irregularity of the teeth or the placement of a mole on a cheek. In a curious way, I began to believe that the dreams were not at all fantastic, but were real memories of genuine events.

"I knew, of course, that there were other children like me. But I began in recent years to seek evidence that there might be even more. And so you saw the newspaper clippings, journal articles, papers on unusual meteor activity in the spring of 1913. I began correspondences with people in distant parts of the country. But, as I said, it all seemed to come to naught.

"That is, until one day, when one of the other wild children happened to send me a photograph of himself. It was an afterthought. He had no particular reason for doing so. But it was a picture of incredible clarity of an adult's face. I knew I had never seen it before, but it immediately struck me as familiar. And then I realized that a younger version of that face inhabited my sleeping world. His was a face in the crowd in my dream."

I was excited, even agitated as Ben told his story. And here I interrupted him to ask impatiently, "Did you ask him if he had dreams similar to yours?"

"Exactly," he said, his eyes gleaming. "And when he confessed that he did, I put together an experiment. I gathered photographs of perhaps 20 of my friends and colleagues. Included were photographs of you and of Charlotte and of Nell as well. And, of course, I included one of my own. And I sent them off to my correspondent. None of the pictures was labeled, and I simply asked him to identify any faces that appeared to him to be at all familiar. I cannot tell you how impatient I was to receive a reply. My friend lived in Colorado. I did not hear from him for weeks. Keep in mind that he and I had never met. I think it unlikely that he would know my face. All the photographs were unlabeled.

"In my instructions, I told him to send back only the pictures that were of faces that appeared familiar. He sent back only two. One was of me, the other of Nell. He had correctly identified the only wild children from a score of photographs. You can imagine my excitement.

"My dreams continued. I suspect that they will be with me all my life. I began to study them even more carefully, to count the faces in them and to mark the configuration of the stars. From that, I learned that I could determine dates and directions, of when we came and when we were to leave again."

He took out star maps over which he had drawn plot lines. He showed me tables of planetary movements. It did not occur to me to doubt him. "What does this mean?" I asked. "What does this tell you about your parents and your birthplace?"

"Only that we were sent here for a purpose, from a place very much like this one. I do not know all the answers. But of one thing I am convinced: we are stopping here on a long journey, one that our children will continue for us. And the charts and tables show that we do not have much time before the planets are in the correct configuration. By next June, we must bring them all together, the wild children and their offspring."

He pointed to the configurations of the stars and planets and showed me his detailed calculations. "This will be the exact alignment of the sky directly above the burnt circle where you first found me, at one hour before noon on the last day of spring next year."

"But you say that this is all based on your dreams!" I protested.

"You are right to question me," he said, running his thin fingers through his gray hair. "It is not the dreams alone. It is something that I know without ever needing to learn it. It is a memory, instilled in here," he tapped his broad forehead. "Perhaps this kind of memory can be passed on from one generation to the next, like the color of eyes, or the curliness of hair. Perhaps they can be implanted there like seeds that only later burst into life."

"What must we do?" I asked.

Ben grabbed my hand. "I knew you would help," he said. "Without you, it would be impossible."

21

Gathering Scattered Flowers

It was a winter of heavy snows and freezing rains. And through this formidable weather, Jackson and I carried out Ben's instructions, sending telegrams and letters, making travel arrangements for families in remote parts of the country, and finally traveling ourselves to distant places to help locate wild children and persuade them to join us in June.

Many of the wild children were dead or seriously ill, victims of the kind of ill health and rapid aging that we had seen in Ben and in Nell. Surprisingly, a number had children of their own.

On a dark winter's afternoon, Jackson and I arrived at the Denver train station to find a city in a white shroud of a blizzard. We had to walk for more than a mile through drifts of snow to a hospital. We followed a nurse to the room where one of the wild children was confined.

"You must not disturb him, and you may not stay long," the woman warned us. Perhaps her sternness should have prepared us, but Jackson and I were startled at the man we had traveled so far to see. His hollow cheeks collapsed with every breath that he sucked into his ailing body. He looked even older than Benjamin. He seemed ancient and was undeniably dying.

His eyes fluttered open when we entered the room and with great effort he lifted an arm and extended it to us. His hand felt like a skeleton's in my own. "I have," he gasped, "been waiting for you." I had to lean over the bed to hear him. "You will take this note to my wife," he said. "I have instructed her to take the children to you in the spring as you have asked."

The air moved into his lungs with a deep moan. "I fear," he said, "I will be gone by then. On a journey of my own." He smiled when the nurse commanded us to leave.

Not all the parents were so easily persuaded, however. After several other stops over the next few weeks, Jackson and I arrived in Seattle to visit with a family that lived on an island in Puget Sound, one that could only be reached by boat. The rain that morning fell in a soft, chilling mist. No one came to the dock to meet us. The man we wanted to see was the husband of one of the wild children, a woman who had died in childbirth. We found him in his house, a huge cabin fashioned from great, round logs. Had it not been raining, I think he might have left us to stand on the porch. As it was, he invited us in to dry off. It was a minimum of courtesy, and he begrudged us even that. At one end of the room we entered was a large fireplace, filled with a stack of burning logs that gave a warm glow to the entire house.

"I have told you and your brother several times that you are not welcome here," said the man. I had learned from Ben that the man's wife had been found almost ten years before on the Olympic peninsula by a small party of elk hunters. She had died five years ago. They had a little girl about Katarina's age, but the child was nowhere in evidence. When I asked about her as Jackson and I warmed ourselves in front of the fire, the man became agitated. "You will never see her," he said. "She is all that I have and I won't let her go off because you have these crazy ideas about her special purpose. Why, you can't or won't even tell me what will happen, or even if I will ever see her again, if I agreed to your scheme."

He seemed hard, even cruel. And I watched him with considerable wariness. On one of the walls I noticed a rifle resting in a rack.

Nonetheless, I began to argue with him, until Jackson interrupted. "It is clear you have made up your mind," Jackson said, gripping the man by the arm. "We cannot force you to agree. We only wanted to present our case and leave it to you to decide. Now that we have done so, we will be on our way."

Jackson let the man go and began walking toward the door, and I followed. The man sat in a chair gazing into the fire, which seemed to freeze rather than warm him. He appeared startled at how easily he had managed to convince us to retreat. And before we had closed the door behind us, he was back on his feet and right behind us. He shook our hands with great vigor.

He was almost jubilant. As we walked back to our boat, he watched us leave. "I wish you success," he shouted after us. "I just can't let her go. Can you understand? I just can't let her."

Seated in our boat, we could still see him standing there. We waved to him. He stood in the frame of the front door, leaning up against the timbers as if he supported the whole weight of the cabin.

22

The Long Journey

Even after Jackson and I returned home, we continued to busy ourselves making the necessary arrangements. There were telegrams to be sent, money provided in some cases, and tickets arranged. I felt as if I were organizing a giant reunion, which in a sense was the case. We were bringing together more than 100 families from around the country, a great gathering of a clan whose seed had scattered and taken root all over our continent.

At times, I felt tormented by this undertaking. Ben had never made it clear what his purposes were, only that the gathering was somehow necessary. Perhaps he did not know. Sometimes I convinced myself that I was part of a vast scientific experiment. We were bringing together two generations of an unusual family, whose strange mental and physical traits were worthy of study. But in my heart I knew that the event we were planning had little to do with science in the normal sense. Rather, it was to be an important moment in history. Not just history on the usual scale of recorded events, but on a larger scale that measured the movements of the earth, the formation of mountains, the origins of life, and the beginnings of the human species.

The spring of 1923 was blighted by an almost incessant rain. We all felt cheated by the gloomy weather, which colored our spirits with its grayness. I had looked forward to romping through the meadows and forest near Father's house with my niece and two nephews. I wanted to show them the ponds and streams where their parents and I had ourselves once played. But that wish had drowned in the continuing rain.

The water and dampness complicated all of our arrangements. We had purchased scores of tents to be put up in the same meadow where we had first sighted Ben. Because of the rain, the temporary housing was wet from the start and quickly showed signs of mildew. Because the ground was so soggy, Jackson led a crew that built wooden walkways all around. A few days of warm sunshine brought flies and mosquitoes, which added to the general discomfort. And then even more rain followed.

I worried about Ben and Nell and the other wild children who would be soon arriving. All but a few were in the poorest of health, and conditions at our tent city might be hurtful to them. Father and Mother promised to help us. I was fearful that Father's skills as a physician would be needed to avoid a calamity.

Yet, as the families slowly began arriving from the

different points of the compass, the adults among them — the wild children and their spouses — were of surprisingly good cheer. Jackson and his crew had constructed a giant cook tent, a framed building with canvas walls. Inside there were long tables and running water and a huge cook stove, which supplied the heat. Within this crudely constructed chamber, where we took our meals together, the gloom of the weather was totally dispelled. Here we exchanged family histories and admired the children. To be sure, there were many woeful stories of lives cut short by illness or limited by physical defect. But there were many more tales of genius and accomplishment. There was the Carolina man who developed a new way to separate metal from ore; a woman from Washington State who identified a parasite that killed bees; and a mathematician from the Midwest who developed a way of mapping time and space on a flat surface. And the children of this generation of physically frail geniuses had the virtues of their parents, but few of the weaknesses. By and large, the offspring were hardy and bright, as strong as they were clever, much like Katarina, Chaz, and Bobby.

Still, they were children and did squabble and, on occasion, even fought, as we spent our days confined to our tents because of the weather. Nell and I played games with the three of them, checkers and chess and memory games requiring a deck of cards. Nell read aloud from a story she was writing, about a planet in another solar system far from our own, where all illness vanished and people lived so long that they could not remember all of their past.

Her hair was white now and there was a slight tremor in her hands. She seemed even older than Mother, whose strength was undiminished and who ruled over the kitchen staff, while Father tended to the sick and infirm of our makeshift community.

On the morning of the planned ceremony, there was a break in the weather. The sun shone through a briskly moving procession of high white clouds and then stood alone, not quite straight above us in a blue sky. Suddenly it seemed that there were wildflowers everywhere, dancing in their brilliant costumes before the light wind and filling the air with the fullness of their fragrance. As suddenly as the weather, my own mood shifted. I felt alone and weary, unprepared for the momentous events that I believed were to come.

The families began emerging from their tents as the meeting time approached. Many of the children ran out into the open meadow to gather up wildflowers and weave them into wreaths more beautiful than any crowns.

"Do not look so somber, Uncle Roger," Katarina said as she danced around me. She kissed me lightly and placed a flower crown upon my head, and I let it stay there. Nell soon joined us, holding Chaz and Bobby by the hand. The boys smiled and laughed and whirled Nell about in circles until she dizzily fell to the ground and begged them to stop.

Soon we were joined by Mother and Father, followed by Charlotte and my brother Benjamin, who hobbled along as well as could be expected with the aid of a cane. His children formed a ring around him and festooned their father with flowers.

We moved slowly over the sodden ground in a growing procession. At the prearranged hour, we gathered at the edge of the meadow. Despite our flower adornments, the adults seemed as serious and somber as we had been cheerful and bright just a day before. Even the children seemed to hold their exuberance in check.

One or two of the parents approached Ben. They shook their heads as they talked to him and then walked away with their children before them, herding the youngsters away from the rest of us. But everyone else stayed on. Those who were walking on canes and crutches now threw them away. Those in wheelchairs stood up and walked. We all moved, slowly and un-aided, into the woods to the small clearing marked still by a burnt circle of ground. The radiating spokes of fallen trees still remained, rotting slowly on the forest floor.

Benjamin moved to the center of the circle. We all pressed close about him, a crowd in the vast wildness of the woods. With great effort, Ben raised his long arms above his head and even the birds grew still. His voice was scarcely louder than a whisper, yet all could hear him clearly. It was as if he were speaking to each of us, one to one. Jackson Stone stood alongside him, as if he could give some of his physical strength to Ben.

"None of us know precisely why it is," Ben said, "but we among the many creatures on this third planet from the sun are part of a great, unfolding plan. We have waited a long time for this moment. And though we have sadness in our hearts, we can all be glad."

He glided out of the center of the circle, moving more easily than he had for years, and found his three children and embraced them. Nell and I took our turns, too, at hugging Katarina, Chaz, and Bobby. To Katarina, Nell gave the little wooden doll that Jackson had carved for her so many years before. I could not stop my tears. The children patted and comforted me.

Katey handed me a handkerchief to dry my cheeks and eyes. "Now, now, Uncle Roger," she said, sounding more the mother than the child. "You must not cry."

Charlotte, who had always seemed the hardiest member of our family, lacked the strength to stay. She kissed her children and then, with Mother supporting her, walked haltingly away.

As the sun reached its highest point in the sky, the children were in place in the center of the little clearing, and we adults formed a circle about them. I felt a contentment at that moment in being with the people that I knew best in the world. We all looked up at once as a cloud suddenly swept across the sun. A cold wind blew over us from beyond the hills, and I felt deeply chilled. My teeth chattered and my limbs shivered from fatigue and the cold.

But the sun broke through again and the breeze dropped. A great column of light fell upon us, heavy as drapery and blinding in its brilliance. I tried to look into the center of the circle but the light was too intense.

I found myself calling out in the midst of an uproar of adult voices, crying out the names of children. I shielded my eyes with a hand and pushed my way toward the center. "Katarina!" I yelled, the name coming from my throat in a cry of pain and terror. "Katarina!" I screamed again with all the urgency of a parent trying to retrieve a child from a burning building.

I walked into a storm of dust and light. Within it I could see the shadowy forms of the children, and among them I thought I could make out Chaz and Bobby and Katarina. I would have kept moving forward, but I was grabbed from behind and thrown to the ground. "No, Roger, you cannot go," said Jackson, who held onto me with that remarkable strength of his. Pinned to the ground, I watched as the earth in the center of the circle seemed to rise up to envelop all the children. The light had become so piercing that I could scarcely keep my eyes open. Yet I could see the shadows of cylinders rising into a fluted column of light and disappearing into the fiery center that shot through a hole in the sky.

With the quickness of a camera shutter, the sky closed up and the light was gone. A strong smell of sulfur and smoke clung to the air. The earth was scorched where the children had stood just a few seconds before. Now they were gone. All save one, who had been pulled from the circle by a tall man who was singed and muddy.

The child, a small boy, beat upon the man with his fists and wailed, "I want to go, too! I want to go, too! Don't leave me behind!"

With Jackson's help, I rose to my feet and found my family. Nell held her arms out to me. She held me as I wept.

"Please do not cry, Roger," she said softly. "Their journey has begun."

23

Reflections

Today I am old by anyone's reckoning. Yet, as many
people like to say with advancing age, I do not
feel old. My health has been good all my life long,
and I have always stayed active. Even now, I keep up
my interest in scientific work, but I leave the hardest
part of the laboratory experiments to much younger
bodies. Working with young people has, I think, helped
keep me alert and, more importantly, occupied. Many
of my best friends have had a habit of dying lately.
And, of course, two of my oldest and dearest ones,
Nell and Benjamin, have been gone a good long time.

It has been my peculiar fate to face old age without
children or grandchildren, or even nephews and nieces,
about me. Charlotte had no more children and chose
not to remarry. In recent years, we have been sharing

the old house where Mother and Father lived for so long. It has been modernized, naturally, but I have taken great pains to keep Father's study just as it was. Today, our little village is little no longer. And the distances have shrunk between the town and the great metropolis to the east. Today it is just a short commute to my office at the university where I continue to teach and study. I try to go there every morning and am still capable of putting in a long, full day.

So you see, in many ways, time has been kind to me. I have been honored beyond what I might have expected or deserved. I have all the money that a man of my age and of regular habits might need. And I still own quite a bit of property, including the old house, which today is close by other, newer, houses. I have many new friends in our village, which has changed greatly, boosted by the growth of electronics companies on the great ring of highway that encloses Boston. Now they make computers nearby, equipment that I never dreamed of as a child and that I still view with considerable amazement.

Yet as I grow older and come closer to my own end, I find my thoughts drawing back to those days with Benjamin and Nell. I spent a good part of my adult life trying to flee from those very thoughts, throwing myself into my work because the past seemed so melancholy and disheartening. I am after all a New Englander, and some of us New Englanders keep our feelings so close that we do not even share them with ourselves.

Now, however, in the mellow years of a long life, I have allowed myself to consider the meaning of my days. And I find a riddle there, an unanswered set of questions about the wild children: Where had they come from? Who were they? Where are they going?

In the attic of our house, I have discovered trunks filled with Ben's books and papers. And little by little I have sorted through them, looking for the answers. Much of what I found were complicated mathematical equations that I have sent off to others to decipher. There are also entire notebooks filled with a strange script, pen scratchings that resemble Babylonian cuneiforms that I shall probably never be able to translate. But fortunately my brother Benjamin also wrote in ordinary English in a diary that he kept quite faithfully from his college days. I started by reading the last entry and then journeyed backward through his time and thoughts to the start.

One brief entry in particular I found to be revealing, and I have read it over and over again. It is dated June 21, 1922 — a full year before the children were to begin their journey. As I read it, I felt as if my brother were with me again, trying hard to answer my questions. On the page is a series of dots and circles in various sizes, some connected by a line. The sketch was similiar to the star map that he showed me a few months later.

"I should have made the calculations before," he wrote. "They are so utterly simple. The earth, the sun, and my guide star, Vega, show the way to yet another star along a straight line in the plane of the galaxy. It is but a faint glimmer to the unaided eye. But there I think, perhaps a century's distance, is home. Maybe one day, rockets can take us there. Yet I believe there is another way to make the journey, blown by winds of light like dandelion seeds on a summer's breeze."

With Benjamin's old telescope, I have scanned the night sky until I have found it. There was no way to know what planets might circle it, what life might flourish, what civilizations have risen and declined.

Nevertheless, I have developed a theory. It is just that and nothing more. It will have to do until there is a fuller explanation, one that could come in a thousand years or so, if I am right. This is my idea:

Long ago on Earth, one of many planets in the universe that circle medium-sized stars, lived a people with a civilization much like our own. There would have to be differences, of course. Perhaps they had no skyscrapers, no engines, no dynamos. Quite possibly there were no televisions, radios, or computers. After all, even our civilization did quite nicely for thousands of years without them. I imagine that they learned to master biological things, just as we have mastered things mechanical. Perhaps they could make the living world do for them what we can only do with brick and concrete, steel and copper and aluminum. Such a people could reach its height and vanish without a trace, leaving no pyramids or highways behind them. Yet like us, they could plot the future of their corner of the universe, calculating the age of the sun and plotting the remote time when life on their planet might not be able to exist. So they created colonies, sending their seed across empty space, like dandelion pods before a summer's breeze, as Ben would say.

But a small colony of humankind might not have the diversity and hardiness needed to survive. These representatives of the human race might grow weak. As their intellect developed, they might become physically frail, prey to the elements, to war and disease. And they would seek a way to renew themselves. One way would be to send a contingent across space to rejuvenate their race.

Not all would survive the journey. Tens of thousands might have begun; a few thousand, perhaps only many hundred, would have arrived. Here they would replenish their kind by marrying into our own, and a new generation would be conceived and grow, strengthened by the mixing of seed. They would leave their mark upon us. Ben's equations would be used to send rockets into distant space. The work of others made it possible to build miniature televisions and computers. Their discoveries simplified the conversion of the sun's energy into electricity and the creation of new varieties of plants and animals. And their friends, too, would be infected by their genius, inspired by their example to achievements of their own.

In time, those who had traveled so far would send their offspring back across space. Not many would go, but enough for a new start. On those who made the return journey, the long journey to a star scarcely noticeable with the unaided eye, could rest the hope for humanity to continue. The hope for our future.

As I say, it is only a theory, perhaps a farfetched one. Yet it is a thought that sustains me in an old age that would otherwise be bleak and lonely. They are probably traveling still, my niece and my nephews, away from the sun, the star that briefly warmed them, past Vega, which guides them, and toward their distant home.

Katarina and Chaz and Bobby and the others are on their journey. They are carrying a small piece of us forward to another place and another time in the history of the universe.

At times I try to think of Katarina waking up on another world, her eyes wide open in amazement and in her hand a little wooden doll.

148

Lately, I have discussed all this with Charlotte. I have given her all of my arguments and explained my theories in considerable detail. She always looks at me in a bemused sort of way that reminds me, as old as I am, that I am her younger brother still.

"You may be right," she said, one recent afternoon, when the first spring crocuses were pushing up their heads through the mantle of old snow. She said it in a way that made it clear that I might also be completely wrong. "For all your theories, we know for certain that we who live on this planet are traveling swiftly through time and space. You could say we were on a journey of our own. We race to an unknown future, all those who have lived and the generations to follow."

And to that I answered, "Yes, dear sister. You are right, and what an incredible adventure this journey will be."

About the Author

PAUL SAMUEL JACOBS is a staff journalist for the *Los Angeles Times. Born into Light,* his first novel, began as a story for his three children. Mr. Jacobs lives near Sacramento, California, with his wife and family.

point

THRILLERS

It's a roller coaster of mystery, suspense, and excitement with **thrillers** from Scholastic's Point! Gripping tales that will keep you turning from page to page—strange happenings, unsolved mysteries, and things unimaginable!

Get ready for the ride of your life!

❑	MC43115-3	**April Fools** Richie Tankersley Cusick	$2.95
❑	MC41858-0	**The Baby-sitter** R. L. Stine	$2.75
❑	MC43278-8	**Beach Party** R. L. Stine	$2.95
❑	MC43125-0	**Blind Date** R. L. Stine	$2.75
❑	MC43291-5	**Final Exam** A. Bates	$2.95
❑	MC41641-3	**The Fire** Caroline B. Cooney	$2.95
❑	MC43806-9	**The Fog** Caroline B. Cooney	$2.95
❑	MC43050-5	**Funhouse** Diane Hoh	$2.95
❑	MC43203-6	**The Lifeguard** Richie Tankersley Cusick	$2.75
❑	MC42515-3	**My Secret Admirer** Carol Ellis	$2.75
❑	MC42439-4	**Party Line** A. Bates	$2.75
❑	MC41929-3	**Prom Dress** Lael Littke	$2.75
❑	MC43014-9	**Slumber Party** Christopher Pike	$2.75
❑	MC41640-5	**The Snow** Caroline B. Cooney	$2.75
❑	MC42456-4	**Trick or Treat** Richie Tankersley Cusick	$2.75
❑	MC43139-0	**Twisted** R. L. Stine	$2.75
❑	MC42968-X	**Weekend** Christopher Pike	$2.75

Watch for new titles coming soon!
Available wherever you buy books, or use this order form.